China and the Jew
Old Civilizations in a

THE JEWISH PEOPLE POLICY PLANNING INSTITUTE המכון לתכנון מדיניות עם יהודי
(ESTABLISHED BY THE JEWISH AGENCY FOR ISRAEL) LTD (מיסודה של הסוכנות היהודית לא"י) בע"מ

China and the Jewish People

Old Civilizations in a New Era

STRATEGY PAPER

by Dr. Shalom Salomon Wald

Executive Report — Annual Assessment No. 1: Between Thriving and Decline — The Jewish People 2004

The Jewish People 2004 Between Thriving and Decline, is the first annual assessment that lays the foundation for professional strategic thinking and planning.

Alert Paper No. 1: New Anti-Jewishness — by Prof. Irwin Cotler — Nov' 2002

The new anti-Jewishness consists of the discrimination against, or denial of, the right of the Jewish people to live, as an equal member of the family of nations.

Alert Paper No. 2: Jewish Demography — Facts, Outlook, Challenges — by Prof. Sergio Dellapergola. June 2003

There may be fewer Jews in the world than commonly thought, and if the current demographic trends continue unchanged, there might be even fewer in the future.

Outline Strategic Paper: Confronting Antisemitism — A Strategic Perspective — by Prof. Yehezkel Dror — May 2004

The increasing ability of fewer to easily kill more makes new antisemitism into a lethal danger that requires comprehensive, multi-dimensional and long-term counter-strategies.

Copyrights © 2004, The Jewish People Policy Planning Institute (Established by the Jewish Agency for Israel) Ltd, Jerusalem

ISBN: 965-229-347-4

Editing: Rami Tal — JPPPI
Typesetting: Marzel A.S. — Jerusalem
Cover Design: S. Kim Glassman, Jerusalem
Printed in Israel by Gefen Publishing House LTD. Jerusalem
WWW.ISRAELBOOKS.COM

CONTENTS

Forword 7

Executive Summary 8
   1. The Emergence of China 8
   2. China and the Jews: Assessing the Current State 9
   3. New Challenges 10
   4. Jewish Policy Responses 11

Policy Recommendations 15

1. Background and Aims 27
   1. Origin and Purpose of this Report 27
   2. Jewish People Policy Goals 28
   3. Cultural Policy as a Means to Strengthen Relations 29

2. The New Context: China's Re-emergence as a Great Power 31
   1. The Power of Culture in China's Long History 31
   2. Long-Term Conditions for Great Power Status: A "Knowledge-Based" Economy ...32

3. Chinese Policy Challenges of the Twenty-First Century Affecting the Jewish People ...35
   1. China's Energy Security and Middle Eastern Oil 35
   2. Trends Towards Increasing Islamic Militancy in China 39
   3. Growing Interdependence between China and the United States 42
   4. The Evolution of China's Relations with Israel 45

4. Beginning Chinese Awareness of the Jewish People 47
   1. Jewish Encounters with China: A Summary 47
   2. Awareness of the Jewish People in Nineteenth- and Early Twentieth-century China ...48

5. Present Judaic Scholarship and its Influence 52
   1. A Narrow Academic Base with a Broad Outreach 52
   2. Who is Advising the Leaders of China? 55

6. Current Chinese Views of Jews and Judaism 59
   1. The "Jew" in Chinese 59
   2. Important Chinese Perceptions 61

7. New Areas of Interest and Old-New Dangers 68
    1. The Relationship with Christianity and the Danger of New Misconceptions 68
    2. The Relationship with Islam and New Moslem Hostility 69
    3. The Growing Shadow of the Intifada and the Chinese Public 71
    4. Western and Japanese Anti-Semitism 73

8. Chinese Dilemmas and Expectations 74
    1. Chinese Policy Dilemmas 74
    2. The Trouble with Kaifeng 75
    3. Other Echoes of Policy Conflicts 77
    4. Chinese Expectations 78

9. Jewish Policy Challenges 82
    1. Possible Policy Dissonances with China 82
    2. Chinese Opportunities and Needs 84
    3. Jewish Policy Shortcomings 85

Annex 1. Questions Asked by Students following S. Wald's Conferences in Chinese Universities,
October and November 2003 87

Annex 2. Titles of Essays on Jewish History and Culture Submitted by Students of the University
of Henan in Kaifeng in Summer 2003 91

Annex 3. Beijing College Students' Understanding of Judaism 93

Annex 4. Sources 105

Annex 5. Acknowledgements 106

Historic Appendix. Notes on Jewish Encounters with China across The Ages 108

Notes 115

FOREWORD

There can be little doubt that China is emerging not only as an Asian power but as a major power on the world stage. China's dynamic economic growth shapes markets worldwide now and in the years ahead will place an increasing demand on oil resources. As Shalom Salomon Wald explains in his excellent paper, China's need for oil will give it an increasing stake in what happens in the Middle East.

But this JPPPI paper is not simply about China's emerging interest in the Middle East. It calls attention to the history of Jewish-Chinese relations. It observes that the Chinese reflect little or none of the traditional forms of anti-Semitism. Ironically, it is Wald's contention that as China opens more to the world and as trade tensions potentially increase, there is a risk that a resurgence of "the old canard of a Jewish world conspiracy" could seep into China. To date, it has not. On the contrary, Wald notes that many Chinese often tend to see the Jews as a mirror of their own history, they admire Jewish wealth and successes, they respect the great contributions that Jews have made to Western civilization (citing most often Marx, Einstein, and Freud), and they perceive themselves and the Jews as representing the "two oldest living civilizations."

Wald also observes that the *Shoah* has become the most widely known episode of Jewish history, and that, too, creates sympathy for the Jewish people. Against this array of positive factors, there is the Intifada and its coverage in China which has begun to affect the good image of Jews and Israelis. The growth of the Muslim population may deepen this trend, particularly as the daily images of violence are, according to this research, "upsetting many Chinese."

With China's increasing significance, this strategic paper makes a strong and compelling case for much greater Jewish engagement with China. Indeed, it makes little sense not to follow this advice. There is something to be gained by building the Jewish relationship with the world's most populous country and something to be lost if this is not done. The paper offers a range of policy recommendations, including the creation of a permanent delegation representing world Jewry to establish an ongoing channel of communication with the Chinese as well as a high level symposium for Chinese policy makers to discuss global issues and mutual relations.

Whether one embraces all of the ideas, the research has clearly identified an area that has been little addressed and that offers important possibilities for the future of the Jewish people. Policy planning should be measured not only by trying to minimize emerging problems but also by taking advantage of potential opportunities. Salomon Wald has certainly met that standard in this paper.

Ambassador Dennis Ross
Chairman of the Board and Professional Guiding Council
The Jewish People Policy Planning Institute

EXECUTIVE SUMMARY

1. THE EMERGENCE OF CHINA

Why China?

China is re-emerging as a great power. This has global impacts in many areas. China's domestic policies and foreign alignments are in flux. Its elites are avidly absorbing new knowledge and are open to many influences. The time to link up with China is now.

Jewish history of the last two centuries was dominated by the fact that until 1939, up to 90 percent of all Jews lived in Europe and America, the two continents that determined the fate of the world. But the *Shoah* and the establishment of Israel have radically altered the geographic distribution of the Jews, and a gradual geopolitical power shift towards Asia is underway. These changes constitute a watershed in Jewish history and open up new opportunities that must not be missed.

Why will China's policies affect the future of the Jewish people?

For the first time, China will directly influence the fate of the Jews. The main challenges that China is facing are not created by Jews but will affect them. Jewish policy makers must put relations with China into a grand strategic frame. Four Chinese policy issues are of great relevance for the Jewish people:

- First, the fast-growing dependence of China on Middle Eastern oil, and that of the main oil producers (Saudi Arabia, Iran) on the Chinese market. Within ten years this trend will overturn the current global strategic equations based on oil. Middle East stability will become a national priority for China.
- Second, the relationship between Chinese Moslems and the Chinese majority (the Han Chinese) that is likely to become more difficult in the coming years. A new militancy can be found among some Chinese Moslems, who feel increasingly close to other parts of the Moslem world. Will China respond to troubles with appeasement, force, or a mixture of both?
- Third, the growing, but potentially tense and unstable economic and strategic interdependence between China and the United States. What role will the American Jewish community play in this complex relationship?
- Fourth, China's relations with Israel, where almost half of the world's Jews live. These relations are important in their own right; they are also affected by each of the first three factors and in turn, will influence them.

2. CHINA AND THE JEWS: ASSESSING THE CURRENT STATE

What is a "Jew" for the Chinese?

In China, the Jews are meeting a great civilization not shaped by Biblical religion or its offsprings — Christianity and Islam. The Chinese can look at Jews with a mindset not conditioned by Christian or Moslem mental baggage: in Chinese, the word for Jew (*youtai*), and its earlier equivalents, has no negative connotation anchored in holy books. This is why a Jewish community could flourish in Kaifeng, the capital of the Northern Song dynasty (960-1126), from the twelfth to the nineteenth century, without encountering religious or political discrimination, and why in the twentieth century, Harbin and Shanghai became havens for tens of thousands of Jews fleeing Russia and Nazi Germany.

When did the Chinese and Jews become aware of each other?

Modern Chinese awareness of the existence of a Jewish people across the world emerged in the 1830s, in the wake of Protestant missionary teachings and Bible translations. Various stereotypes then took form, including that Jews were victims of the "white man" like the Chinese themselves. In the early 1920s, the founder and first president of the Chinese Republic, Sun Yatsen, justified his public support for Zionism with this perceived affinity between the two peoples.

In the twentieth century, Jewish scholars contributed to a broader appreciation of China in the West, but Jewish leaders paid little attention to China, with the major exception of David Ben-Gurion, who alerted Jews to the importance of relations with the great civilizations of Asia, particularly China.

Who teaches the Chinese today about Jews and Judaism?

After the Cultural Revolution (1976), a new generation of Chinese Judaic scholars began to satisfy growing Chinese curiosity about Jews and Israel. They are few in number, and active in less than a dozen universities and academic centers. Their outreach is vast, through teaching, workshops, hundreds of books and articles, and exhibitions. Scholars are also likely to play an important advisory role on Jewish and Middle Eastern issues for China's leaders, most of whom are today university graduates themselves. However, academic work is constrained by financial limits, lack of internal and external cooperation, and some political restrictions. The broader Chinese public gets its information on Jews and Israel from television, movies, and increasingly, the Chinese Internet. Many appreciate the latter as an alternative source of information that, although it can be censored, is less uniform and controlled than the official media.

What are the main Chinese perceptions of Jews and Judaism?

What the Chinese see in the Jews has often been a mirror of their own history, their fears, dreams, and desires. First, many Chinese have an image of great Jewish wealth and success that they admire and would like to emulate, although this image may be partly unrealistic. Second, they note the great contributions Jews have made to Western civilization — Einstein, Marx and Freud are often quoted names. Third, a regular comment is that the Chinese and Jews represent the "two oldest living civilizations," a comparison that indicates respect for the Jewish people's historic continuity. And fourth, the *Shoah* has become the most widely known episode of Jewish history. Millions of Chinese have seen *Schindler's List* or related movies.

3. NEW CHALLENGES

The first years of the twenty-first century have seen new areas of interest emerge in China, particularly the relationship between Judaism and its two "daughter" religions, Christianity and Islam. The popularity of Bible stories and Christian beliefs seems to be growing; some young Chinese ask questions about Jesus and why the Jews don't recognize him. In parallel, and spurred by current events, there is a new interest in the historic relationship between Judaism and Islam and the origins of the current antagonism.

Another challenge might arise from China's opening to the world, which will allow foreign anti-Semitism, in its various old and new disguises, to seep into the country. Trade tensions with the West, or Middle East hostilities, might raise the old canard of a "Jewish world conspiracy" in China, as occurred in Japan in the 1980s.

The growing shadow of the Intifada

The Palestinian Intifada has begun to affect the positive image of the Jews — or the Israelis — in the eyes of the Chinese. For the first time, questions are being asked: Are Jews and Israelis the same people? The official, public position of the Chinese government is sympathetic to the Arab cause, and the media reflect this. State-controlled television shows the Middle East conflict in a prominent, often one-sided fashion. The daily images of violence are upsetting to many Chinese, particulary Chinese Moslems. Experts have begun to report a fundamental change, a radicalization of Chinese Moslem attitudes to events in the Moslem world. This has added to internal tensions in China, as it has in some European countries.

Chinese policy dilemmas

Like many countries, China grapples with conflicting policy objectives. It needs to accommodate the Arabs and the Jews, Third World countries, and the United States, and at home, the rich and the poor provinces. Policy dilemmas explain some of the Chinese hesitations and censorship with regard to Jews, Israel, and the Middle East. Some officials and advisors want better relations with the Jews or Israel, others are cautious or hostile. But there is undoubtedly great public interest in these issues, and an unsatisfied need for more and better information.

What do the Chinese expect from the Jews?

There is no formal Chinese "wish list," but many Chinese seem to believe that Jews could do something for them, because of their perceived global influence and their long historic experience:

- The most often expressed hope is that the Jews will help China manage and improve its difficult relationship with the United States.
- There is continuing respect and demand for Israeli technology.
- Middle East stability or instability, and Israel's role in it, is a source of nagging concern.
- Some Chinese would like to understand and emulate the perceived business success of the Jews, and their international connections and performance in science, technology, and innovation.
- More Jewish support for Judaic studies and publications in China is expected.
- Some think that the modernization of the Jews, and their role in the modernization of the Western world, might provide some useful lessons for China as well.

4. JEWISH POLICY RESPONSES

Why has the Jewish response been insufficient?

Jewish policy responses to Chinese opportunities and interest have been insufficient. There has been a shortage of vision, information, coordination and money. It is true that Jews have had many short-term problems that were much more urgent. But it is also true that the Jewish people have lacked long-term strategic perspectives and in general have had no long-term policies. Also, Jews are not a coherent unit, but a complex, multinational, self-organizing people with many cooperating but also competing branches and bodies.

Like the Chinese, the Jews will face policy conflicts: strengthening relations with China might clash with the policies of the United States, as has occurred in the past. For some Jews, human rights concerns and the Chinese reluctance to grant minority status to the Jewish descendents in Kaifeng, might become other bones of contention.

What should be the Jewish policy goals?

None of these potential problems should impede efforts to pursue key Jewish policy goals, which are:

- Strengthening the links between China and the Jewish people and broadening China's knowledge of Jewish culture and history, to facilitate a better understanding of current events;
- Responding to false stereotypes imported from abroad;
- Emphasizing common interests and perspectives between the Chinese and Jewish peoples, including shared geopolitical and other global concerns.

Policy recommendations

No single policy can respond to all these goals, but a mix of policies might. This mix should include approaches to decision makers and communication with scholars and students-members of future elites — as well as with a broader public. The consent of Chinese authorities and experts will obviously be essential. It must also be understood that this is a long-term endeavor; not everything can be implemented quickly. But it is important to make a start now, taking up at least some of the following recommendations:

1) A permanent delegation of main Jewish organizations speaking for large parts of the Jewish people

Because there is no indigenous Jewish community, no Chinese citizen can speak on behalf of Judaism or the Jewish people, in contrast to Chinese Moslems and Christians. The State of Israel cannot and should not represent the entire Jewish people. A permanent delegation of World Jewry, maintaining relations with the appropriate Chinese government authorities and institutions, should help improve information flow between China and the wider Jewish world, as well as mutual understanding and cooperation. Such relations do exist between Jewish organizations and other countries and continents.

2) A high-level symposium for Chinese policy makers on shared global issues and mutual relations

Visits between Chinese and Jewish leaders have in the last three years been less frequent than before. There is a need for high-level discussions and analysis of the changing world situation, and of shared concerns and mutual interests. This need should be met by more high-level visits, but also by an initial joint symposium of policy makers, advisors, and experts. If this is successful, more regular symposia could follow, focusing on other emerging global issues and additional subjects of interest to China and the Jewish people.

3) A symposium for Chinese business leaders on entrepreneurship and innovation

Beyond the technological cooperation and trade between Israel and China, the international connections of the Jews of the world, and their experience in research, innovation, and the development of a "knowledge-based" economy might be of interest to China.

4) Training courses for university teachers

Courses on Judaism for university teachers and authors of history textbooks have helped improve the knowledge of Judaism among students. Efforts to familiarize university teachers with the basic facts of Jewish culture and history must be strengthened.

5) An academic Judaism center in Beijing

China is the only one of the "Five Big Powers" of the United Nations that has no academic institute on Judaism in its capital. The main institutes are all in the provinces. A Judaic institute near the political centers of power seems increasingly necessary.

6) Support for scholars, students, and joint academic seminars

The most common forms of academic cooperation are support for scholars and students, including short- or long-term study visits, and support for seminars. These must be strengthened, with particular attention to the need to help a small number of young Chinese to reach an international level of Judaic scholarship, e.g., in ancient or modern Hebrew.

7) Publications, books, translations

There is considerable Chinese demand for written information on Jews, Judaism, Israel, and the Middle East. The writing and translation of books should be better funded, and the availability of publications made more widely known. A list of five hundred essential Jewish books to be translated into Chinese should be drawn up. Additionally, China's popular magazines could be encouraged to publish articles on Jewish themes.

8) A Web site on Jewish history and culture

A Chinese Web site on Jewish history and culture, maintained on the index page of one of the main Chinese search engines, might have great success with the fast-growing number of Internet users. Among young Chinese, this was the most popular of all recommendations. Another computer-related recommendation is to produce or help distribute DVDs with Jewish themes.

9) Television documentaries

TV documentaries are watched by hundreds of millions of Chinese. More on Jewish themes should be shown, and new ones produced in a form that is adapted to Chinese audiences. One very popular topic, for example, is new agricultural technologies from Israel.

10) Jewish film festivals

The successful annual Jewish Film Festival in Hong Kong should be brought to Beijing and other cities as well.

11) Public exhibitions

A recent (2004) Chinese proposal to have an exhibition on Jewish culture, held in one of Beijing's main museums, should receive a positive response.

12) Jewish donations

A brochure summarizing memorial events, and donations made by Jews to the Chinese people, might show a measure of Jewish gratitude for the safe haven many of them received in China in the twentieth century.

13) Improving the Jewish people's understanding of China

Strengthening the links between two peoples is a two-way street. This report examines one of these ways: how to strengthen the Chinese understanding of the Jews. The other direction — how to improve Jewish understanding of China — is no less important and must be explored further.

POLICY RECOMMENDATIONS

The following recommendations are the outcome of the reflections of this report. They contain responses to the identified policy needs and shortcomings, but also offer new initiatives.

One of Confucius's disciples once asked the master to define the essence of his teaching in one single word, to which he answered: "Reciprocity". If one had to summarize all the following recommendations for strengthened links between China and the Jewish people in one single word, it would be: communication, better communication. In order to communicate better, and also gain China's consent and cooperation for such an endeavor, something beyond more visits or money is necessary: a vision and long-term policy strategy such as the Jewish people have rarely had.

In regard to China, a long-term policy strategy will require at least three steps:

- A definition of the difference between Jewish people and Israeli state policies. Obviously, the two are not the same, although sometimes they will be closely coordinated and often, cooperative. This report deals with Jewish people policies.
- An indication of the specific tasks of the main branches of the Jewish people. With regard to China, American Jewry is clearly of paramount importance (Chapter 3.3). American Jews are able to achieve things that no other branch of the Jewish people can achieve.
- A priority-setting mechanism, or at least an agreement on major priorities. This is a difficult step. Priority setting and a comparative cost-benefit analysis of recommendations are essential for a rational policy, but they are sensitive and often politically impossible or irrelevant because independent decision makers and funding sources will do what they consider most important.

No single policy will address all identified needs and opportunities, but a mix of policies could. The recommendations identify media, institutions, and one-time events that could be instrumental. Their effectiveness and practical as well as political feasibility have been discussed with Chinese and Jewish experts. Many recommendations incorporate their advice, and are also guided by the success of past experiences; after all, a lot has already been tried and achieved in China. The recommendations address various audiences and have different time perspectives:

- Aecommendations for the short term, addressing high-level and policy-making audiences: 1, 2, 3
- Recommendations for the medium term, addressing larger, including popular audiences: 1, 7, 8, 9, 10, 11, 12
- Recommendations for the long term, addressing China's future elites: 1, 4, 5, 6, 7, 8

In general, the cost-effectiveness of these recommendations is likely to be high; Chinese salaries and costs, including inland airfares are still very low. All or nearly all recommendations could probably be carried out over a period of five to ten years with an annual budget of approximately U.S.$ 1 million in addition to what is being spent by various sources today, except perhaps for the first recommendation, which will require international salaries.

The most difficult task will be to choose between different activities that are competing for limited resources. There is no objective, rational method to choose, for example, between short-term, high-level political approaches and long-term efforts to inform China's future elites. Would it be more productive to have two or three leading Jewish policy makers visit China for a couple of days for discussions with senior Chinese officials, or to have three important Jewish books translated and printed in Chinese for scholars and students, in editions of three to five thousand copies? The financial implications would be of the same order of magnitude for both options — approximately U.S.$ 20-30 thousand — but does it make sense to compare the two, and who can say which would yield more lasting results?

It must be understood that this is a long-term endeavor. Not everything can be done simultaneously and at short notice. But it is important to make a start now and maintain a medium- and long-term agenda of those recommendations that cannot be carried out immediately. If budget or political considerations call for initial limitations, four recommendations should be taken up first and foremost (although other experts may have different priorities): a high-level seminar for policy makers (1), a new Web site (8), university teacher-training (4), and publications and translations (7).

Whatever the activities, all should be carried out with the knowledge of the appropriate Chinese authorities and in partnership with Chinese institutions and experts.

RECOMMENDATION 1. A PERMANENT DELEGATION OF MAIN JEWISH ORGANIZATIONS SPEAKING FOR A LARGE PART OF THE JEWISH PEOPLE

Rationale

Some Chinese experts have indicated that they prefer initiatives towards strengthening the relations between China and the Jewish people as a whole, Israel included, over one that aims at Israel only. Together, World Jewry may be able to exert a stronger leverage than Israel could do alone. The different branches of the Jewish people have different perspectives and to a large degree, independent policies, but they can also act as a cooperative and complementary body.

China presents a unique situation, unknown in any other important country that is not hostile to Jews. The absence of accepted, indigenous Jewish communities that could represent the Jewish people and create a counter-weight to its opponents, as they do in the Americas, Europe, Russia, South Africa, and Australia, leaves a void. The Chinese, including Chinese Moslems and Christians, are free to state their views — and if they wish, their criticism — of Judaism, while no official Jewish voice is able to reply. For example, some Chinese Moslems see themselves as representatives of the world of Islam, not only of Chinese Islam. They can successfully protest against scholarly publications if these contain theses on the relations between Islam and Judaism that are not condoned by Moslem clerical authorities (Chapter 7.2). China's foreign Jews cannot reply, lest they be suspected of contravening Chinese laws, which prohibit religious propaganda by foreigners. Well-meaning Jewish visitors who wished to fill the void, have argued in high places for other perceived Jewish interests. Such interventions should be part of a coherent and agreed strategy.

Ways and means

It is proposed that international Jewish organizations begin to coordinate policies and discuss the possibility of setting up a small, permanent office in China, with a delegate who could speak on their behalf. Setting up such an office will require the agreement of the Chinese authorities. It should have quasi-formal relations with the Chinese government or appropriate official associations and institutions. Political hurdles will have to be overcome both among Jews and in China. To the Jews, it must be made clear that this delegation is not a new political body with independent functions, but an extension of the cooperation that existing organizations are already carrying out with other countries and continents. To China it must be made clear that the delegation does not represent a "Non-Governmental Organization" in the traditional sense, but an office with some political status speaking for at least part of World Jewry. The delegation must maintain contact and information exchange with the local Jewish communities (Beijing, Shanghai, Hong Kong) and make sure that its work does not impinge on existing agreements between the Jews living in China and the authorities. Also, close contacts should be maintained with the country's Judaic scholars. The responsibilities and bureaucratic reporting lines of the delegation will require consideration and agreement. This office should have several tasks:

- Enhancing the existing information-coordination between the Chinese authorities and the wider Jewish world, on cultural as well as geopolitical and other issues of common interest.
- Strengthening cultural and scholarly relations between China and the wider Jewish world.
- Following Chinese media reports, publications, and student books relevant to the Jewish people; reporting to Chinese and Jewish authorities any old or new misconceptions and expressions of prejudice or hostility affecting the Jewish people as a whole, particularly when they have an obviously foreign origin.
- Following general public attitudes to Jews and Judaism as far as they can be assessed. One way to do this would be by Internet opinion polls, which have already been used in China for commercial purposes.
- Maintaining contact with journalists and media commentators.

RECOMMENDATION 2. AN INITIAL HIGH-LEVEL SYMPOSIUM FOR CHINESE POLICY MAKERS ON SHARED GLOBAL ISSUES AND MUTUAL RELATIONS

Rationale

Mutual visits between Chinese and Jewish policy makers have probably been less frequent since 2000 than before. There have been many personal changes in the political leadership of China and the wider Jewish world, which means that the two sides may now be much less familiar with each other than they were before. Chinese and Jewish leaders are aware that they are facing critical long-term choices in a complex and often dangerous international environment. These choices do not only relate to politics and security, but also to economic, environmental, and cultural issues. There is a need for policy makers and advisors from both sides to get better acquainted with their respective views, be it on mutual relations or on global issues that are important to both.

Ways and means

It is proposed to organize a first symposium for high-level Chinese policy makers, advisors, and experts, attended by counterparts from the Jewish world. It should include a small number of selected participants, last from two to five days, and remain off the record. The themes of such a symposium should cover the role of China and the Jews in the changing geopolitical environment of the twenty-first century and Chinese-Jewish relations, and might include future Chinese roles in the Middle East. It would also provide an opportunity for both sides to discuss their respective concerns.

If this symposium is successful, it could be followed by others, perhaps focusing on wider global problems not specific to Chinese and Jews, and/or on historic and cultural questions that are specific to Chinese and Jews, such as the issue of modernizing ancient civilizations.

In addition to symposia, study tours for Chinese officials and policy advisors to major Jewish communities in the world, including Israel, should be encouraged and financially supported.

RECOMMENDATION 3. A SYMPOSIUM FOR CHINESE BUSINESS LEADERS ON ENTREPRENEURSHIP AND INNOVATION

Rationale

There is an economic dimension to "Jewish culture," in the broad sense of the term as it is used in Chinese (Chapter 1.3). This dimension is important in the present context. The most pressing concerns that preoccupy a large majority of Chinese and the Chinese state will for a long time remain economic: they are concerned about poverty and how to make ends meet. The Chinese public is fascinated by the stereotypical rich Jew, but does not understand the basis for Jewish wealth. Some Chinese repeat worn-out Western clichés about Jewish domination of the stock market, the banks, etc. (Chapter 7.4). Intellectuals do not necessarily understand the issue much better.

Jewish economic success in history was and is mostly based on combinations of international connectedness, risk-taking, knowledge, and scientific-technological skills. The Jewish lead role in the high-technology sectors of several countries is well known. Chinese leaders have recently expressed again their appreciation of Israel's competence in the high-technology areas. During an official visit of Israel's minister of industry, trade, and labor in June 2004, China's minister of science and technology, Xu Guanhua, said that his country was "committed to building a long-term, mutually beneficial cooperative relationship with Israel, so that China may boost its international competitiveness and its ability in risk management."[1] While state-to-state cooperation in technology trade and investment is not a subject of this report, it is suggested that the global experience and advice of Jewish business entrepreneurs, executives, and innovators from high-technology sectors could be utilized to make a positive contribution to China's long-term economic development — experience and advice in which China might show interest. It should not be difficult to mobilize the interest and cooperation of at least some important Jewish entrepreneurs outside Israel. However, this proposal is tentative, and its details will have to be further discussed.

Ways and means

- One way to explore whether and how China could benefit from the international experience of Jewish entrepreneurs, particularly in the creation of a knowledge-based economy, is to organize a public symposium for Chinese business executives, public officials, and economic journalists, with appropriate Jewish participation. A positive side effect of such a symposium might be in helping to correct some of the popular simplistic clichés about Jewish riches.
- It might be useful to set up a more permanent administrative structure for continuous discussions and better networking between Chinese and Jews, perhaps a Chinese-Jewish technology and business advisory council.

RECOMMENDATION 4. TRAINING COURSES FOR UNIVERSITY TEACHERS

Rationale

Many people receive their first knowledge of foreign countries and cultures — and lasting positive or negative stereotypes — through schoolbooks and teachers. Chinese elementary school texts contain little on Western history, and nothing on Jews, according to information provided by Chinese scholars who were consulted. However, university textbooks, particularly on history or religion, do contain references to Jews, not all of them positive (Chapter 7.1). One of the most efficient ways to reach large numbers of students is through training courses for university teachers and researchers. Three such courses were organized over the past years by the University of Nanjing, and a few in earlier years in Shanghai. The Nanjing courses were intensive one-week classes, attended altogether by more than one hundred university teachers. These courses were considered a great success, and stimulated interest in other universities as well. They have already led to changes in history books by authors who had participated, who subsequently eliminated erroneous and unfriendly comments about Jews or added new paragraphs or chapters on Jewish history in their books.

Ways and means

Teacher-training courses must be continued and increased. It is important to:

- Find reliable, multi-annual funding sources;

- Organize such courses in a number of universities.

RECOMMENDATION 5. AN ACADEMIC JUDAIC STUDY CENTER IN BEIJING

Rationale

China is exceptional in that its main centers of Judaic scholarship are all located in the provinces, not in the capital. The need for a Judaic scholarship center in Beijing is keenly felt. Geographic and personal proximity to the centers of political power and decision making often increases the influence of academic scholars and advisors. Establishing such a center will require an official Chinese partner. The CASS (Chinese Academy of Social Sciences) Institute of World Religions has indicated interest in building such a center and is searching for Jewish partnership, but other academic institutions have shown interest too.

Ways and means

It should be a Jewish policy goal to help set up an academic Judaic center in a Chinese institution in the capital, and to have a Jewish academic institution from the United States, Europe, or Israel (or a consortium of several of them) act as a counterpart and participate in its work. Jewish representatives should discuss the most appropriate location with the Chinese government. One of the first goals should be the creation of a comprehensive Jewish library in Beijing.

Another, more permanent, form of academic cooperation could also be achieved by setting up a binational or bicultural foundation, to be financed equally by China and Jewish organizations, with Israeli academic participation. It could be called the "Sino-Jewish Foundation" and function similarly to the binational foundations already set up between countries, such as the United States and Israel. There are other models that could be examined for their adaptability to Chinese conditions.

RECOMMENDATION 6. SUPPORT FOR SCHOLARS, STUDENTS, AND JOINT ACADEMIC SEMINARS

Rationale

Scholarships, student exchanges, study tours, and joint scholarly seminars are the bread and butter of cultural and academic cooperation. They are essential. Little will be added here because all four policies have been supported for many years, involving China, Israel, and other countries interested in Sino-Judaic relations. (International seminars on Chinese and Jews have been held in the United States and Germany as well). Policy makers are aware of the importance of these policies.

However, there are some particular needs and opportunities that must receive special consideration.

First is the need to train the next generation of Judaic scholars for China. Very few Chinese scholars, including one or two Christian clergymen, have an advanced knowledge of Hebrew, ancient or modern. It is doubtful whether there is more than one or two who master the language of the Bible to the degree that would today be expected from Judaic scholars in the West. However, a small number of Chinese graduate students in China, Israel, or other Western countries could reach this level if they were given time and more support.

Second, new methods are needed to attract Chinese undergraduate students to Jewish topics. Particularly interesting are essay competitions for students on Jewish history and culture. The Institute of Jewish Studies of the University of Henan in Kaifeng has so far organized two essay competitions on Jewish history and culture (in summer 2003 and spring 2004) in order to encourage Chinese students to take up Judaic studies. Modest rewards (a small sum or a book) were offered to the authors of good papers, and their names were published in the university journal, together with the titles of their essays. In 2003, forty essays were submitted from across the campus, not only the Jewish Studies Institute, and thirty received prizes. In 2004 the number of participants rose to ninety-eight (for details see Annex 2). This seems to reflect the enduring popularity of the Jewish topic among some young Chinese students.

Third is a need to give some priority support to scholarly interests that have been stimulated by current events, such as research on the history of Jewish-Moslem relations, or the origins and history of anti-Semitism. Apart from individual scholarships, joint academic seminars might discuss these and other issues. The issue of how to modernize an old civilization is one of these, which, if not taken up by policy makers and advisors (see Recommendation 2), should at least become a joint academic research theme. Another issue is the relationship between mainland and overseas Chinese, which can be compared with the relationship between Israel and Diaspora Jews. There are indeed interesting parallels but also differences between the Chinese and Jewish experience.

Ways and means

- Support for scholars, students, and joint academic seminars must continue and be strengthened, giving priority to studies that could lead to a better historic understanding of current events.
- A few advanced Chinese students and scholars must be helped to reach an international level of scholarship in Hebrew and Jewish studies. They could become the nucleus for the next generation of Judaic scholars in China.
- Kaifeng's successful essay competition for students on Jewish history and culture should be continued and the concept introduced in other universities as well. There are other institutes of higher learning in China where similar student interest might be found.

RECOMMENDATION 7. PUBLICATIONS, BOOKS, TRANSLATIONS

Rationale

The importance of this recommendation cannot be overestimated. It addresses China's future political, economic, and cultural elites. China is still a book-reading country, as it has been during past centuries. Hundreds of books and articles on Jews and Israel have appeared in China over the last twenty years, but the demand for information has never been satisfied because the print runs were too small or the public did not know of these books or where to get them (Chapters

8.3, 9.2). Translations from foreign languages are particularly important, but nobody has a comprehensive translation plan or list of priorities for China. It is essential to get more books out to the Chinese public, in larger numbers, and make their availability more widely known.

There is a particular need for objective, scholarly books on the origins of Christianity and Islam and their first links with, and later antagonism to, Judaism. The history of Jews under Islam, the sources of the Arab-Israeli conflict and the history of Western anti-Semitism are subjects related to current events that interest many Chinese readers. Another perennially topical theme is the role of the Jews in Western economic history, and a more recent issue of great interest, particularly among female students (who are a majority in Chinese universities), is the position of women in Judaism and Jewish history. The old and recent history of Jews in China also attracts curiosity and should be better known in China. There are many books in Western languages on these subjects, but few have been translated into Chinese.

Ways and means

The following initiatives should be considered:

- Have a small group of recognized Jewish and Chinese scholars publish a list of five hundred essential Jewish texts that should be translated into, or reprinted in Chinese. This list alone would have a big impact on Chinese scholars and publishers. A first step towards this list would be an inventory of Chinese books and articles on Jewish topics, including translations that have appeared from the 1970s on. Various scholars have produced partial, not published inventories, but these must be compared, integrated, and updated. This would be a significant, maybe long-term, but increasingly important task.
- Write or translate short, popular introductions to Jewish religion, culture, history, etc. There is a great, unfulfilled need for simple, easy-to-read books, in parallel to scholarly works.
- Provide small subsidies to encourage authors of Judaic books, and pre-publication subsidies for publishers who often hesitate to bring out new books without prior financial guarantees.
- Announce the publication of new books and inform where they can be bought, on a new Jewish culture and history Web site (see Recommendation 8).
- It is difficult or impossible to place articles on Jewish topics into Chinese daily newspapers. However, there are a number of popular magazines interested in short stories about foreign events, cultures, etc. It might be possible to publish informative articles on Jews and various aspects of Jewish history and culture in such magazines.

RECOMMENDATION 8. A WEB SITE ON JEWISH HISTORY AND CULTURE

Rationale

The importance of the Web keeps growing by the day. It will be one of the most important sources of information and for many young Chinese, particularly students, it is already. There are approximately 80 million Chinese

Internet users (mid-2004), a figure that is increasing by at least 30 percent annually. Each day, some 10-20 million users visit the main Chinese Web sites. There are several Web sites on Jews or Israel, but they are limited, often local and little known. The creation of a nationally known Chinese Web site on Jewish history and culture would be timely and popular: in discussions with Chinese students, this proposal has met with more enthusiasm than any other. Chinese policy advisors and experts also search the Web for information on Jews and the Middle East.

Ways and means

The server hosting the material on Jewish topics must be in China. It would not be a difficult task to find appropriate material on Jewish topics in existing Chinese publications, as well as Chinese students and scholars who would agree to write or translate small articles at short notice for Web pages.

The following steps should be followed:

- Find a Chinese partner, preferably one of the three most important Chinese portals/search engines: *sina.com*, *sohu.com*, or *China.com*. This partner must keep "Jewish Culture and History" on its index page, lest the existence of the new site will remain unknown.
- Discuss the financial and political conditions with the managers of the engine (if the public interest is large enough, hosting the site could be cost-free). The managers are fully informed of possible constraints.
- Identify Chinese volunteers to establish, maintain, and update the new Web site.
- Get a few Chinese scholars or institutes to make regular contributions. Scan books and articles to be shown on the Web site.
- Provide an initial twenty to thirty Web pages, including one on new Chinese books on Jewish topics, providing information on how to acquire them (see Recommendation 7).
- Include one page with information on young Jews who are looking for Chinese pen friends. Chinese students, particularly in Judaic study centers, would like to have Jewish pen friends but do not know how to locate them.

RECOMMENDATION 9.
TELEVISION DOCUMENTARIES

Rationale

Television documentaries are very popular and are watched by hundreds of millions of Chinese. In April 2004 there were thirteen central national channels, not to speak of hundreds of local channels, and the number keeps growing. Chinese Central Television (CCTV) Channel 1 has the broadest outreach and is followed all over China. CCTV 10 shows programs on science and education, CCTV 7 is a military channel, and a new channel was recently created for children. *National Geographic* and American World War II documentaries seem to be very popular, among others. Many Chinese have learned of the *Shoah* through television. CCTV is said to be short of interesting Jewish documentaries in Chinese, or with Chinese subtitles.

Many college students watch DVDs on their computers. For them, DVDs are more important than television.

Ways and means

A greater effort should be made to show the Chinese people more documentaries on Jewish history and culture, as well as Jewish contributions to China. CCTV may accept some assistance in identifying and locating Jewish documentaries adapted to Chinese audiences. A subject that is of enormous interest both to China's leaders and a large majority of the population is Jewish inventiveness, as expressed in Israeli agricultural technologies, including drip irrigation, solar energy, and more. Many Chinese farmers know of Israel, appreciate that these Israeli innovations have helped to improve their lives, and would like to hear more about this subject. Chinese leaders know the potential political power of their 800 million farmers, and have become very attentive to their wishes.

Again, as with the proposed Web site, the financial and political conditions of showing documentaries must be discussed with the managers of CCTV.

DVDs with Jewish themes should be more widely available for students, in addition to TV documentaries.

RECOMMENDATION 10.
JEWISH FILM FESTIVALS

Rationale

Largely unknown on the Chinese mainland, the Jewish Community Center of Hong Kong has organized four Jewish film festivals, one every year since 2000.[2] The fifth festival is planned for November 2004. All festivals were accompanied by audience awards, press releases, and radio interviews, and had public success widely beyond the Jewish community. The sponsors included private donors, industrial companies, and the consulates of the countries where these Jewish films were produced: Austria, Canada, France, Germany, Israel, Italy, Poland, and the United States.

Ways and means

The Hong Kong Jewish Film Festival merits support and publicity. Its success should be emulated in other places in China, particularly in Beijing. There, different political and practical conditions will have to be met, e.g., receiving approval of the Ministry of Culture and/or the mayor of Beijing.

RECOMMENDATION 11.
PUBLIC EXHIBITIONS

Rationale

Exhibitions have had an important place in Jewish cultural outreach to China. There have been exhibitions on the *Shoah*, on the Israeli-Palestinian conflict, on Israeli design, on individual Israeli painters, on the Jews of Kaifeng, among others. Nearly all of these were local and limited in time. Few if any had a national echo. This is why some Chinese experts have questioned the cost-effectiveness of local exhibitions, which generally require substantial effort in time and expenditures to organize. Moving exhibitions could alleviate this shortcoming but would also be more expensive. Public exhibitions can make Jewish history and culture better known to sections of the Chinese people, and thus are an alternative to movies, Web sites, and books.

Ways and means

- In spring 2004, a Chinese institution proposed to host an exhibition on Jewish culture that would be organized with Israeli participation. As this would take place in one of China's most important national museums in Beijing, it could become an important event, of a different class and with potentially wider impact than earlier, more limited exhibitions.
- To improve the outreach of this as well as other exhibitions, it is essential that the local and national Chinese media, particularly television, report the event. In the past, the media have often ignored exhibitions.

RECOMMENDATION 12.
JEWISH DONATIONS

Rationale

Scholars in Beijing and Shanghai have suggested that Jews make a charitable gesture in China, in recognition of the fact that many Jews found refuge there before and during World War II. It was said that this would impress the Chinese public and be remembered. The idea that Jews have never made a charitable contribution in China is wrong, and Chinese disappointment is unjustified. There have been Jewish donations in Hong Kong, Shanghai, and in a rural area of the Guangdong province where a foreign Jew built a dormitory and other facilities to help poor local children get education, food, and medical care. There might be more that are not known. Some contributors may not wish to publicly flaunt their generosity and prefer to remain discreet.

Ways and means

It would be useful to carry out a review of Jewish donations and charities made for Chinese people in the twentieth century. The results could be published in a brochure, which should also indicate where new charities would be particularly welcome. It is known that Jews in some Western countries such as the United States, give substantially more charity for non-Jewish than Jewish causes.

RECOMMENDATION 13.
IMPROVING THE JEWISH PEOPLE'S UNDERSTANDING OF CHINA

Rationale

Strengthening the links between the Jewish people and China has to be a two-way street. This report discusses only one way, i.e., the means to improve the Chinese understanding of the Jews. How to improve Jewish understanding of China is an equally important matter that awaits further work. Here we can only emphasize the importance of the issue. The Historic Appendix to this report shows that Jews have had fleeting cultural encounters with China across the centuries, leading in the twentieth century to strong scholarly and popular Jewish interest in and sympathy for China's modern history and civilization.

Ways and means

It would be easier to make policy proposals for Israel than for other parts of the Jewish people. In 2004, five to six hundred Israeli students were studying the Chinese language or history at the universities of Jerusalem, Tel Aviv, and Haifa, which is an impressive number considering Israel's size. The general public's interest in China has been reflected, among others, by the huge success of the Israel Museum's Chinese art exhibition in 2001, so far the largest ever held in Israel. But in Israeli school education, Asian history is still marginal — a fact that should be corrected. The general interest in China should also be encouraged by means of more translations of Chinese books into Hebrew, public lectures, exhibitions, and film festivals.

To evaluate the current Jewish interest in China in other countries is extremely difficult: it is probably much higher in the United States and Australia than in Europe, both among Jewish leaders and intellectuals and in the general public. American Jewish scholars and writers have written a large professional literature on China. What still seems to be missing among Jews is a more general awareness of the needs and opportunities for closer links between China and the Jewish people.

Background and Aims

1. ORIGIN AND PURPOSE OF THIS REPORT

Why does China's future impinge on the future of the Jewish people? Jewish fate of the last two centuries was dominated by the fact that until 1939, up to 90 percent of all Jews lived in Europe and America, the two continents that determined contemporary and Jewish history. The annihilation of most European Jews and the creation of Israel have reduced this figure to less than 60 percent, but apart from Israel, the eyes of the Jewish people remain fixed on Europe and America and their culture and policies. Yet it is now urgent to recognize that there is "a global power shift in the making":

> The transfer of power from West to East is gathering pace and soon will dramatically change the context for dealing with international challenges — as well as the challenges themselves. Many in the West are already aware of Asia's growing strength ... Asia's growing economic power is translating into greater political and military power.[3]

As China, the first Asian country, is on the way to becoming a great power again, Jews will have to give greater attention to their relations with it. China's foreign policy will become more assertive, not only in China's immediate neighborhood, but on the world scene. Chinese strategists see their interests more and more akin to those of other great powers, rather than the Third World, and will demand the right to "share global responsibilities," to quote Chinese officials.[4] Jewish policy makers have come to appreciate since 2000 how much Jews depended on the support of a single superpower. In a strategic vision of the future, the new emerging powers, particularly China, must loom large. A geopolitical shift towards Asia could constitute a watershed in Jewish history. It will offer opportunities to improve the future of the Jewish people. Compared to these opportunities, the risks are few. New geopolitical conditions must be explored and used. It would be irresponsible not to do so.

Jewish policy makers were not always sufficiently alert to China. Many Jews know that during World War II, Shanghai was home to more than twenty thousand Jewish refugees from Europe. Few know that many more could have been saved there had they only known that this safe haven existed, and had Jewish leaders done all they could to bring them to Shanghai. Tragically, several of these leaders did the contrary, not because they lacked compassion or a will to help, but simply because China was outside their mental universe and did not belong to what they believed to be the "civilized" world. Today, it is deeply troubling to discover their deliberate efforts to stop the emigration of Jews from Central Europe to Shanghai when their rescue was still possible, and to read the quote of a senior board member of the *Reichsvertretung der Juden in Deutschland* ("Reich Representation of Jews in Germany") who in 1938 to 1939 still resisted pressure to transport more persecuted Jews to China although they had nowhere else to go:

> It is more honorable [*sic*] to suffer a martyr's death in Central Europe than to perish in Shanghai.[5]

Jewish policy makers and the Jewish public must grasp the new challenges and opportunities presented by China's emergence now, not in twenty years. For this, Chinese and Jews must become more aware and better informed of each other.

2. JEWISH PEOPLE POLICY GOALS

The goals of a Jewish policy with regard to China can be summarized as follows:

i. The main goal is to strengthen the links between China and the Jewish people, improve the Jewish people's standing and the goodwill towards it, and broaden the knowledge of its history and culture, so that the Chinese might gain a better understanding of current events. This might also allow for a better understanding of Israel as the state of the Jewish people, and of Israel's goals and predicaments. To this end, easier access to information about Jewish history and culture would be required, through teaching and research, books, movies, television, Chinese Web sites, and exhibitions, in response to the interest that is often shown by the Chinese public.

ii. A part of the above-mentioned goal is to spread the knowledge that relations between Chinese and Jews are very old, that Jews have come to China in peace and friendship at least from the times of the Tang dynasty on (618-907 C.E.), and that a Jewish community in Kaifeng in the Henan province played a small but distinguished role during eight centuries of Chinese history. Also, Chinese interest in the twentieth-century history of the Jewish communities in Shanghai and Harbin should be further encouraged.

iii. In China as in other countries, there are stereotypes about Jews. Some are false and a few are hostile. All have been imported from the West, the Moslem world, or Japan. Correcting and if possible, eliminating negative stereotypes is another Jewish policy goal.

iv. In the longer term, when China will share more global responsibilities, a further goal is to have China acknowledge the global challenges and regional dangers facing the Jewish people, and show awareness that China and the Jews may share major geopolitical concerns, internationally and regionally. A Chinese expression of this awareness might by itself, have a geopolitical impact.

3. CULTURAL POLICY AS A MEANS TO STRENGTHEN RELATIONS

This report postulates that cultural policy can be a key instrument in strengthening future relations as a whole. The Chinese have always had great respect for culture, and the meaning of the term in Chinese is very broad. "Culture" (*wenhua*) occupies a central place in Chinese thought, and has more dimensions than its English equivalent. It includes not only the arts and letters, but also language, the essential symbols of life, the patterns of behavior, the shared and written heritage. The Chinese traditionally attribute great power to culture, particularly the "capacity to affect others by other than military means."[6] In other words, *wenhua* embraces all the meanings of "soft power," to use the terminology of modern political science. China's ruling dynasties liked to emphasize their role as protectors of the country's cultural tradition. Even in the twentieth century, one of China's most traumatic upheavals was called the "Cultural Revolution" (1966-1976), although the origin and goal of this event were political.

Presenting the Jewish people in its cultural forms means to recognize the centrality of cultural and intellectual endeavors in China's history and thought. A "cultural policy" might open more doors between the Chinese and the Jews, increase the flow of information, enhance the mutual understanding of both peoples' history, and create awareness of communalities and shared concerns. Can cultural policies circumvent short-term political difficulties and lay the basis for improved long-term relations, including relations in political areas? Is this assumption valid for China? The Chinese do differentiate between the cultural and political spheres, and while they may be tolerant of cultural and religious manifestations, they can also become suspicious when the latter appear to involve politics. This is why some Jewish experts have had doubts: culture is an instrument of Chinese government policy — it could not, on its own, modify relations between peoples. A few Chinese expressed the same doubts, or hostility to efforts to improve relations in general. However, the majority of Chinese experts have supported the basic assumption that cultural relations are a key factor in building future relations as a whole, and many students who may have fewer vested interests in the academic standing of Judaic studies than their professors, have agreed enthusiastically. But China is not monolithic. It will be important to engage both supporters and possible opponents of increased links in further discourse.

The principal target groups for cultural policy in the broadest sense are, obviously, the "elites" — intellectuals, opinion leaders, decision makers, teachers, and students. This does not mean that the broader public should be ignored. Many less educated people in China have heard of the Jews or Israel. Some ways and means of conveying more knowledge are accessible to everybody, not only to the elites. There are many vehicles to spread information and, no less important, to spread emotions, i.e., sympathies and antipathies. There are lectures and seminars, newspapers, books, movies, television, DVDs, radio, Internet, exhibitions, and cartoons. There are popular songs, including the lyrics of pop singers and rock bands, which are very popular among China's youth. There are sermons in mosques, churches, and temples, there are public speeches given to crowds through loudspeakers, and the list could go on. In any event, the means of spreading information are changing fast. Radio, which played a vital role in the 1950s and 1960s, seems to be disappearing in China too — except for those who want to listen to foreign stations. Newspapers are less important than in the past — few students read China's dailies. Rock bands were unthinkable in China thirty years ago, when information and emotions were conveyed to many people by loudspeakers in May Day parades. Today, the latter has become rare. Therefore, the modes of cultural contact must be continuously adapted to changing realities.

This report relies heavily on scholars, experts, and universities as sources of information. Scholars create and transfer a great amount of knowledge, particularly to the power elites. Scholar-officials ruled China for more than two thousand years — intellectuals who had to pass the grueling academic examinations by which imperial China chose its office-holders. After an interruption of several decades, scholars seem to be emerging again as policy advisors to decision makers. Academic teachers were relatively easy to approach for this project, as were many other sources. A detailed list of sources is provided in Annex 4. This report, particularly its policy recommendations, goes beyond academic teaching and books, and the recommended cultural policy is embedded in and interacts with a broader policy context.

The New Context: China's Re-emergence as a Great Power

1. THE POWER OF CULTURE IN CHINA'S LONG HISTORY

China has been a great power — culturally, politically, and economically — much longer than any other living civilization. It exercised lasting influence on countries near and far for the better part of the last two thousand years. China was still a great power, on a par with any Western country, as late as the eighteenth century. It was a centrally ruled, self-assured empire of approximately 300 million inhabitants, while France, England, and North America were home to 20 million, 10 million, and 6 million people, respectively. Its army controlled large parts of Central Asia, its domestic economy was stable and prosperous, its great art was still innovating, its neo-Confucian philosophers were commentating on the classical texts, and its silk, porcelain, lacquer, and tea were exported to every corner of the world. What eighteenth- and nineteenth-century China failed to develop, in spite of its great scientific and technological achievements in earlier centuries, were the modern sciences and technologies. That finally precipitated old China's defeat and demise. Historians have discussed the cultural, economic, and political reasons for this monumental failure ever since.

But in terms of China's long history, the interval between the last period of imperial glory and power, and the present time is very short.

What distinguishes China from other great powers? One difference is the length and apparent continuity of its history in the same country. Another is its periodic rise and fall. The main dynasties of the last two millennia, the Han, Tang, Song, Yuan, Ming, and Qing saw China's power rise, peak for one or two centuries, then recede, battered by foreign invasions and internal rebellions, only to rise again after an interval of weakness and fragmentation.

A third difference that may also explain the first two, relates to the cultural, immaterial foundations of power. The longevity of China did not depend on the Chinese state, which was often shaky, nor on the ruling dynasties, which rarely achieved complete unification and territorial control for more than limited periods and had no reliable local power base. Nor could it depend on the force of arms alone, because no army was able to permanently keep together a country as vast as China. Leading sinologists have explained the continuity of Chinese civilization in various, complementary ways. J. Fairbank and M. Goldman speak of China's "social institutions" and "behavioral patterns" that "are among the oldest and most persistent social phenomena in the world."⁷ These social institutions and patterns of behavior are integral parts of "culture," as the Chinese understand the term. They were indispensable to the statecraft that allowed China to manage a population and country of a size unmatched in human history. Pierre Ryckmans explains why "China is the oldest living civilization on earth": her "unique continuity" is based on a "cult of the past in Chinese thought" and a sense of history that is entirely based on spiritual memory, language, and the written word, not on the material monuments that have nearly all been destroyed and rebuilt many times. What distinguishes China is the "spiritual presence and physical absence of the past." Ryckmans adds an observation that is particularly relevant to this report:

> Only the Jewish tradition may present a significant parallel to the phenomenon of spiritual continuity, which I am trying to study here.⁸

Few other Westerners have noted this parallel of "spiritual continuity," but some Chinese intellectuals have seen it. It explains some of their interest in the Jewish people (Chapters 4.2, 6.2).

As China continues to modernize, the future evolution of its cultural tradition is unpredictable, and so is that of the "behavioral patterns" that have, until recently, helped to maintain China's continuity. Underneath the ongoing Westernization of all fields of life, many Chinese patterns of behavior and thought remain molded by Confucian and other old traditions. However, these are no longer integrated into a dominant and over-arching value system that China could invoke or propagate, like traditional Judaism or Islam. China's justified pride in its great, old culture is unlikely to restore the old, and has not yet created a new value system.

2. LONG-TERM CONDITIONS FOR GREAT POWER STATUS: A "KNOWLEDGE-BASED" ECONOMY

China is re-emerging into a position of great power, which it lost almost two hundred years ago. Its current re-emergence, however, occurs under circumstances that never existed before. Economic globalization is transforming China into the world's main manufacturing center, and an indispensable trading partner for more and more companies and countries. The industrial contribution to China's gross domestic product rose between 1990 and 2002 from 42 percent to 52 percent, which is a unique trend.⁹ In all more-developed countries, the industrial contribution to GDP is declining rapidly. Experts agree that China's economic development from the early 1980s on has been more impressive than had been anticipated. A French think tank predicted in May 2003 that by approximately 2050, Europe's share in the world economy might sink from 22 percent to 12 percent, and that China's share would rise to 25 percent,¹⁰ still less than the Chinese share in international trade in the eighteenth century, estimated to have reached 38 percent. However, international and Chinese experts agree that the country's successful incorporation into the world economy will raise huge domestic policy challenges and may call for difficult political decisions.¹¹

Since the 1980s, China's emergence as an economic powerhouse has been unparalleled in speed and size. This will open up a potentially enormous market, but will also impose painful adjustment processes on many other countries and sectors. It will have long-lasting ripple effects across the global economy. It is in China's interest to associate thousands of foreign companies with its development. This would alleviate, but not eliminate, the adjustment pains, which are likely to lead to a period of domestic political backlashes in the West against China. Politicians will have to cope with such repercussions, the first signs of which have already appeared in Europe and the United States, where China has become the second-largest trading partner. In 2003, China overtook Mexico, providing 11.4 percent of all US imports, and its trade surplus with the United States amounted to $124 billion. Painful adjustment processes have been a trademark of the last 150 years of world economic history, but they were either imposed by industrial countries on underdeveloped, rural and often colonial economies, or they occurred between industrial countries. The Opium Wars against China in the 1840s are an example of the appalling adjustments imposed on a weak country, whereas the industrial expansion of Germany before World War I and that of Japan after World War II are examples of major adjustments within the industrial world. China is the first case of a still relatively poor country that is imposing large-scale adjustments on both the industrialized and industrializing world, becoming in turn one of the biggest importers of raw materials. The picture becomes even more complex if one considers that this development is the result of global market forces rather than power politics, and that much of it is steered by foreign multinationals. In 2003, foreign-funded enterprises accounted for 55 percent of all Chinese exports. We have no historic model to predict how the necessary global adjustments will be played out.

China's current economic strength is its ability, utilized by the multinationals, to manufacture whatever the world market wants to buy and to do this more competitively than anybody else. But this cannot remain forever the only basis of the country's strength. Chinese science, technology, and industry must in the long term become more innovative if the country wants to keep up and compete with progress elsewhere. In the long term, China too must become a "knowledge-based economy." China's leaders know this; they are convinced that science and technology are the drivers of the future. This explains the impressive growth of Chinese research and development (R&D) expenditures, increasing between 1991 and 2002 by 15.2 percent annually in real terms. In numbers of researchers China has now overtaken Japan (811,000 versus 676,000 R&D personnel), although there are differences of definition between the two countries. However, this remarkable effort was not matched by a comparable increase in scientific and technological productivity. Looking at patent indicators, which are the best available measure of technological innovation, China is lagging behind by a large measure. Its innovative performance or R&D output bears no comparison to its R&D expenditures or input. In 1999, China accounted for less than 0.2 percent of the world's patents (half of which were owned or co-owned by foreign companies or persons), whereas the US, the EU, and Japan together accounted for more than 90 percent of the world total.[12]

There are several reasons for China's scientific and technological lag. First, there has not been enough time to reap the benefits of recent R&D. Other reasons are: poor intellectual property protection; the legacy of a heavy economic planning system that relies on state-owned enterprises and politically appointed managers; and the absence of links between industry, university, and government laboratories.

Some Chinese and Chinese-born scientists have begun to critically analyze China's "low scientific profile on the world stage," which one of them attributes to the "Confucian tradition of respecting customs and hierarchy", "political conformity", and "deference to authority and to existing paradigms [which] is a major barrier to scientific breakthrough."[13] These scientists have research experience in the United States and know that in the West, scientific and technological innovation requires an open society that allows for independent thought and free circulation of ideas. However, the question remains whether these Western characteristics can easily be introduced into China without jeopardizing the stability and cohesion of this huge country. China is said to have "the world's longest tradition of successful autocracy,"[14] and was often suspicious of novelty. Ever since the nineteenth century, spanning three generations, Chinese intellectuals have been wrestling with the question of whether "modernization" must necessarily mean "Westernization." Many young city dwellers believe that it does, which is why their conscious cultural models are Western. Chinese intellectuals have been looking for models of modernization in many directions, East and West. Japan, Korea, and Singapore, not unlike China, have been controlled societies that share with China some post-Confucian characteristics. Over the last thirty years they have developed a more significant capacity of innovation. But China does not depend on foreign models only. Thanks to its prolonged internal modernization debate, "China is able to look to its own past for ideas, if not answers."[15]

This Chinese modernization debate shows parallels to the one that began among European Jews one hundred years earlier, initiated by the Jewish Enlightenment, when Jews were exposed to the same pressures of Western thought and civilization that later threatened to overwhelm the Chinese too. In the twentieth century, the outcome of these debates varied widely between the Chinese and Jews, including in the fields of science and technology. Sigmund Freud and others explained the extraordinary contribution of Jews to the scientific revolution of the twentieth century by their tradition of "creative skepticism." This is the opposite of the "deference to authority and to existing paradigms" that has now been criticized by Chinese scientists.

But that criticism alone may indicate progress towards a new Chinese form of "creative skepticism," which was, in fact, a well-known quality in ancient Chinese philosophy. It could be a sign of reforms to come.

Chinese Policy Challenges of the Twenty-First Century Affecting the Jewish People

China's rapid economic expansion and its growing geopolitical weight have led to a number of Chinese policy challenges, some of them completely new. Jewish policy makers must keep these challenges in mind. Jewish people policy cannot change China's basic geopolitical context, and must not conflict with China's vital national interests. China's development in the next twenty years will face challenges that do not depend on and are not linked to the Jewish people, but China's policy responses could profoundly affect Jewish interests. It is essential to understand these challenges and analyze whether Jewish policy could have at least an indirect influence on them or on Chinese responses, or whether Jews could adjust to them. This will call for long-term strategic thinking by Jewish policy makers and the incorporation of Jewish policies into a grand strategic frame.

The four most important factors that will determine Chinese policy in areas of major relevance to Jews are:

- The fast-growing — and for the next twenty years probably irreversible — dependence of China on Middle Eastern oil, which will begin to overturn the current global strategic equations based on oil by 2010.
- A possible trend towards increasing Islamic militancy, and violence between Moslems and Han Chinese in China's heartland.
- The growing economic, scientific-technological, and strategic interdependence between China and the United States, and the possible Jewish influence on it; as well as the danger of future trade and military tensions.
- The future evolution of China's political, economic, military, and cultural relations with Israel. These will, to some degree, depend on the preceding three factors, but also on proactive Israeli and Jewish policies and information efforts with regard to China.

1. CHINA'S ENERGY SECURITY AND MIDDLE EASTERN OIL[16]

Oil is becoming the single most important determinant of China's Middle East policy. China's continuous economic growth depends on fast increases of oil imports. In 2003, China overtook Japan as the world's second-largest oil consumer: almost 5.5 million barrels per day

(6 million in early 2004), compared to more than 20 million for the US. From the early 1990s on, China's oil demand kept growing faster than that of any other country. Even so, China today is still a diminutive oil user (7 percent of global oil consumption) because its per capita demand of oil is very small (e.g., only one tenth that of South Korea). But the oil thirst of this giant economy will be enormous, and long-term oil demand is predicted to increase steeply to respond to the fast growth of transportation, power generation, and petrochemical production, regardless of whether there is a temporary cooling of the Chinese economy. Of China's consumption in 2003, two of the 5.5 million barrels per day were imports. As domestic production will not go up, the rapid consumption increase must be covered entirely by imports: China's oil demand in February 2004 was 33 percent above that of March 2003, its crude oil imports 60 percent above. Thus, China is on the way to becoming, in the not so distant future, the world's second-largest oil importer after the United States. If trends continue, its imports could approach those of the United States in the years after 2020. It is estimated that by 2020, 75 percent of China's oil needs will be covered by imports, and 90 percent of these will come from the Middle East.[17] Changes in the composition of energy sources and greater energy efficiency can, in the coming years, have only small effects on the overall picture, because oil represents no more than 7 percent of China's power generation and 19.5 percent (2002) of its total energy mix, with coal already providing 69 percent of power generation and 58 percent of the total primary energy supply.[18] New energy technologies would have to be developed and made competitive very quickly if they are expected to substantially modify the energy balance within the next twenty years. This would require an enormous international research and development effort that is, unfortunately, not in sight. China's biggest oil supplier is Saudi Arabia, followed by Iran and then West Africa. China cannot avoid growing dependence on Saudi oil because Saudi Arabia alone is considered to have the reserves and the capacity to respond to China's oil needs. Oil experts agree that China's frenetic efforts to diversify its supplies will lead only to minor, not major reductions of this dependence.[19]

For Middle Eastern oil producers, the geopolitical change that is underway, is inverse but equally dramatic: East Asian countries and particularly China will not only be their largest and most profitable markets (companies sell oil in Asia at higher prices than elsewhere), but they could also become the countries with the biggest direct stake in the political and social stability of the producers. China is likely to remain the oil market with the largest annual growth for the next twenty years; Saudi Arabia needs this market and treats China with great care, deploying intense efforts to secure for itself the largest possible Chinese market share, which is very revealing. China's new oil dependence is radically different from Europe's traditional vulnerability and dependence, particularly that of the 1970s and 1980s. This time, the oil producers compete with each other and understand better how much they need their consumers for investment, safe long-term markets, and political and other protection — at least as much as the consumers need the producers. China knows that it deals from a position of strength, and that the producers are being careful not to upset their most important customer. This is why China can continue to take a very restrictive view of, for example, Saudi or Iranian requests to open more consulates or organize "culture weeks" in China. If American pressure for the democratization of the Middle East continues, the "flight" by Middle Eastern autocracies to find safe markets and protection in China is likely to accelerate. Yet this position of relative strength cannot obscure the fact that oil security, both in the sense of security of supplies and supply routes, is already a source of nagging concern for China.

Some of the world's geopolitical equations will be overturned and replaced by new ones that are not yet clearly visible. For example, the level of interdependence between the Middle East and East Asia may become greater than that between the Middle East and the industrialized Western countries. Chinese observers have already noted that China's new energy balance might increasingly influence the political and economic dynamics of the Middle East, as well as the relationship of the Middle East with the rest of the world. It might be only a question of time before China and perhaps Japan and Korea too, will begin to question the claim by Western, particularly European nations that they have a preferential and historically "privileged" link with the Middle East.

The basic data are not controversial among specialists, but the changes have been too fast for the public and the politicians of most countries to follow. In China, central planners and Party officials had known for some time that the ideal goal of complete energy independence could not be achieved if the country wanted to maintain high growth rates. They did not anticipate, however, that their dependence would grow so fast and become so large, because market forces and not government policy drove both the speed and size of the change. The new situation, which is rarely, if ever, discussed in public, is said to have created considerable unease in government circles. The growing dependence has major policy implications that are slowly sinking in; Chinese advisory bodies and think tanks are now discussing China's long-term economic, environmental, regional, technological, defense, and foreign policy options, and it is the latter two that are of particular interest in our context.

China's immediate issue is how to protect its energy security. China will have several options, none of them easy or assured of success. One option is to go it alone, trying to get preferential treatment from oil-rich countries by supporting all their political and military aims, including a renewal of the weapons sales of years past. This is the least attractive, and for China under current circumstances, the least likely option. It could not guarantee security and stability, but would guarantee a sharp increase in tensions with the United States and draw China into a labyrinth of intrigues and antagonisms between Middle Eastern producers. However, if tensions with the United States increase for other reasons, the go-it-alone strategy might become more attractive again. A second option would be the opposite: to work closely with the foreign and security policy of the United States in trying to stabilize the Middle East. This is currently a difficult-to-imagine break with China's official position, although the Chinese cannot ignore that the United States Navy already guarantees the security of the long-haul sea transport of oil from the Middle East to the Far East, which will be irreplaceable for many years to come. In the medium and long term, the American option could become increasingly inevitable if China's vital interests cannot be better protected by multinational cooperation. For the time being, it is the latter option that seems to have China's favor. A leading Chinese energy expert and government advisor recently proposed an innovative and unexpected version of multinational action. He suggested that China move towards an "East Asia Energy Security Cooperation," including Korea and Japan. East Asia (China, Japan, Korea) is now the largest oil-consuming region of the world, with almost 30 percent of global demand. Led by China, this group would soon represent a formidable economic and political power:

> East Asian countries, with a growing common interest in stabilizing oil markets and politics in the Middle East, should have a common strategy towards the region, including on such issues as the Israeli-Palestinian conflict, Iraq, religious extremism and terrorism.[20]

In November 2003, it was announced in Beijing that China, Korea, and Japan were planning to "establish a unified energy market," which could be the first step towards an energy security cooperation. This cooperation, however, has so far been hampered by intense rivalry between China and Japan for priority access to the big Russian oil pipeline under construction.[21]

Permanent instability in the Middle East is fast becoming a threat to China's and East Asia's economic success and could one day even be a *casus belli*. Since Islam began to penetrate China from the eighth century on, no event in the Middle East, and no export from there, has ever touched upon China's vital interests in the same way. The situation is now radically different. Until recently, the Chinese could decide their policy mix for the Middle East without endangering their own vital interests. This mix consisted of vocal (and modest material, including military) support for Arab causes, and close and mutually beneficial relations with Israel in several fields. China's new situation must, over time, prompt major policy reassessments. China will be faced with questions that are no longer ideological and diplomatic but have become existential. These questions have preoccupied Westerners before: Is it possible to settle the Arab-Israeli conflict now, "once and for all," to quote a former Israeli prime minister, and thus inaugurate a long period of peace and prosperity, or is it only possible to better manage this conflict? Which configuration between Israel and Palestine, which kind of Palestine, will foster stability? How will the evolutionary potential of a Palestinian state affect its neighbors, particularly Saudi Arabia? How realistic is the assumption by some Chinese policy experts that Saudi Arabia will remain a stable and reliable oil exporter for the next twenty or more years, maintaining normal relations with the United States? And if not, what options will China have?

The implications of China's oil dependence for the Jewish people do not have to be negative, particularly if Israel is seen as contributing to, and not jeopardizing Middle East stability. China's mind is not yet made up with regard to the Middle East, and its elites are still learning. But China's own analytical potential to comprehensively examine these and other related questions, even though it is growing, is still limited. Some important Western publications on Islam, the Middle East, or Saudi Arabia are either not, or not easily available, in China, or they are not known to some Chinese Middle East experts. But some Chinese scholars look at these issues with a strong sense of history, which might give them a broader vision of the present and the future. One Chinese expert commented that the Chinese must study Jewish history and culture in greater depth than before, and this for a topical political reason:

> We must use our own perspectives, otherwise we will never be able to develop an original policy in the Middle East — you can't always borrow from others.[22]

2. TRENDS TOWARDS INCREASING ISLAMIC MILITANCY IN CHINA

The history of Islam in China is proud, culturally rich, and politically complex. Arabs entered China's coastal and probably also northern cities as peaceful traders in the eighth century, if not before. They entered Central Asia as warriors in 751, when an Arab-Moslem military alliance defeated the army of Emperor Xuanzong of the Tang dynasty in the battle of Talas River. The Chinese defeat was a watershed in Asian history and contributed to the destruction of Buddhism in Central Asia, Afghanistan, and present-day Pakistan, and its replacement with Islam. China stimulated the curiosity of many early Arab and Persian scholars and travelers. It is from Arab historians of the ninth and tenth centuries that we have the first detailed reports about Jews in China.[23]

Over the centuries, Sino-Islamic relations have known periods of quiet as well as hostility. During the Mongol Yuan dynasty, many Central Asian Moslems settled in China and played privileged political, economic, and military roles. They kept political power and influence during the Ming as well, and enjoyed an expansion and revitalization in the seventeenth century, following more intense contacts with the rest of the Moslem world. Many Moslems integrated into Chinese civilization, to the point of adopting traditional Chinese temple architecture for some of their mosques, but without abandoning essential elements of their cultural-religious heritage. In contrast, the nineteenth century saw bloody Moslem revolts in several parts of China, which were severely repressed. For instance, in the province of Yunnan a Chinese Moslem scholar started a rebellion and in 1856 established an independent Islamic state that survived almost sixteen years. Since its creation, the People's Republic of China has endeavored to establish peaceful relations with its minorities, particularly to satisfy the socioeconomic and many of the religious aspirations of the Moslem population, while apparently also constraining some religious freedoms and suppressing particularistic political aspirations. The Chinese rulers, not unlike emperors of earlier dynasties, used written history in selective ways to enhance peace and stability. Chinese schoolbooks did not mention the battle of Talas, or they embellished its true outcome. In line with modern Moslem Chinese historiography, the Moslem rebellions of the nineteenth century that are still remembered in some provinces, are officially presented as proto-Communist revolutions against "feudalism" and "exploitation." Although it cannot be denied that they had an important socio-economic component, these were also revolts against Chinese rule and civilization. Over the centuries, the Chinese state has never succeeded for any length of time to isolate its Moslem population from the spiritual and political trends of the wider Moslem world.

Moslems live and travel across the entire territory of the People's Republic of China. No outsider has a comprehensive view of the current state of Sino-Islamic relations in this vast land. Because the subject is so sensitive and little reported, even the Chinese authorities may not always have a fully comprehensive picture. Officially, of a total population of 1,340 million Chinese, more than 20 million are Moslems, of which 11 million live in the Xinjiang province. Unofficial figures that cannot be substantiated speak of 35 million or more Moslems. In any event, the Moslem population constitutes a smaller percentage (less than 3 percent) of the total population than nearly anywhere else in Asia, Africa, or Europe. Certainly, there are happy, professionally successful, and well-to-do Chinese Moslems, a fact that Chinese writers like to emphasize, occasionally with some exaggeration.[24] On the other hand, it is no secret that relations between Han Chinese and Moslems, whether they are Uighur speaking (Xinjiang province) or Chinese speaking (Hui minority), have recently become more difficult. Concerns about the future are rising. A Moslem American scholar complained that Chinese Moslems are, in her view, discriminated against and embittered, and that they suffer from a general Chinese prejudice. She cited what she considered to be the most common Chinese stereotype of Moslems, that they are "an inherently violent people."[25] As if to confirm her testimony, a former senior official in the Chinese Bureau of State Security is quoted as saying on 25 December 2001 to an American policy expert of Saudi origin:

> Islam is arguably the most dire threat to Chinese national security and national internal cohesion today ... Thus, what comes out of Saudi Arabia will be one of our main dilemmas of the future ... We also have a deep fear of their ever growing and immense influence in the Islamic world.[26]

This alarmist statement was certainly influenced by the events of 11 September 2001. But not long after, Bernard Lewis predicted that the world of Islam, if it adopted extremist fundamentalist views, would start to clash not only with the West, but with its other neighbors as well, such as China.[27]

In 2003 a traveller could learn of bloody incidents between Moslem and Han Chinese that had occurred in various provinces of China (the autonomous region of Xinjiang is not included in this observation). These incidents were not reported by the media. Some Han Chinese are expressing their hostility to Moslems in terms similar to the stereotypes just quoted, or worse. In short, there is a problem, which in the eyes of some Chinese, is getting worse. There are many reasons for this problem. One is that many Moslems live in the poor, western regions of China, where unemployment is high and levels of education low. Another is that many Moslems feel increasingly linked to the wider Moslem world. China has, unintentionally, encouraged and accelerated this trend by allowing its state-controlled television to give the Palestinian Intifada and the war in Iraq great prominence, and to present both in a pro-Arab light. Moreover, China has allowed its television viewers access to Al Jazeerah news via Chinese television summaries, following the opening of an Al Jazeerah bureau in Beijing in November 2002. In France, similar policies by the state-influenced media from 2000 to 2003 have not appeased French Moslems, but emboldened and enraged them. As an unanticipated side effect, this has helped to trigger an unprecedented anti-Semitic, and also anti-French, campaign in France itself, largely instigated by young Moslems. There are many indications that at present some Chinese Moslems are equally enraged. Foreign experts have begun to report a fundamental change, a radicalization of Chinese Moslem attitudes to events in the Moslem world. While the first Gulf War of 1991 and earlier Arab-Israeli clashes are said to have created little more than a stir, the Iraq war of 2003 and the Palestinian Intifada are intensely watched and bitterly resented as wars against Islam itself.[28]

An increase in personal and religious links between Chinese Moslems and the Middle East is influencing this change. According to official Moslem statistics, there are today 45,000 imams, 35,000 mosques, and 26,000 Koran students all over China, most of them in the Xinjiang province. Few other religions in China, if any, can boast such figures. In addition to these statistics, an unknown number of Chinese Moslems are studying with the encouragement of China's Moslem authorities in the *medresses* (Islamic schools) of Iran, Saudi Arabia, Egypt, Pakistan, and Syria, and a growing number of Moslems join the *hajj* to Mecca. Whatever other constraints China may impose on its Moslems, no other religious community seems to enjoy comparable freedoms. A vice-president of the China Islamic Association, who mentioned the countries above, added that the young men studying there would be the "future leaders" of China's Islam. Was this policy unavoidable in view of internal or external pressures? The official brochure of the China Islamic Association, "dedicate[d] to the 1,350th Anniversary of Islam's Transmission to China," emphasizes the overriding importance of Islamic education, but also shows, in words and pictures, the solidarity between the leaders of China's Islam and visiting leaders of Iran, Saudi Arabia, Libya, the PLO, and others.[29] Watching daily events elsewhere in the world, it would not be unrealistic to fear growing Islamic militancy and violence in China in the coming years. Chinese experts are aware of the problem but are confident that China will know how to cope with it. China's leaders and elites want their country to coexist peacefully with the Moslem world, particularly with China's Moslems. China's official Moslem authorities welcome this wish. Perhaps China is not yet prepared for a possible reversal of Moslem attitudes, away from coexistence and towards religious and political militancy.

Sino-Moslem tensions could affect China's policies towards the Middle East and the Jewish people. The Chinese might give greater vocal or other support to the Palestinian cause, for the same reason many Westerners do. To quote Bernard Lewis's sarcastic words: "Westerners … tend to give the greatest importance to those [Moslem] grievances, which they hope can be satisfied at someone else's expense."[30]

But China's relations with Islam have not

been burdened by a long history of conflict and recrimination comparable to the conflicts between the West and Islam. Ancient China was tolerant of — or indifferent to — religious diversity. Occasional clashes with Islam were, on the Chinese side, not motivated by religious antagonism, and Moslems could follow their religion and participate in public life. It is true that expressions of cultural distaste for Moslems could sometimes be found in ancient China, for example contempt for the Moslem prohibition of pork, but this is a far cry from Europe's outright enmity. China, in contrast to Westerners or Mongols, never threatened or colonized the core region of Islam, the Middle East (although the Qing dynasty re-occupied parts of Moslem Central Asia in the mid-18th century). It was Islam that penetrated China and tried to convert the Chinese, sometimes with success.

Therefore, China may feel less compelled to appease "Moslem grievances" than Westerners. China might even recognize that it shares geo-strategic problems with the Jews. Perhaps both sides could benefit from their mutual experiences. It is not inconceivable that this might facilitate a future Chinese peace-supporting role in the Middle East (Chapter 3.4). Chinese policy makers and experts are watching Israel's relations with other important countries that are relevant to the Moslem world. Chinese policy experts, and probably leaders as well, still consider India a potential rival, and were apparently taken aback in 2003 by the public display of close, and in particular military, relations between Israel and India. India strengthened its relations with Israel notwithstanding its own Moslem population of 150-200 million, which is many times larger than that of China. China will certainly pay close attention to the future evolution of Israeli-Indian links, particularly after the Indian elections of spring 2004, which brought a new government to power under the Congress Party.

3. GROWING INTERDEPENDENCE BETWEEN CHINA AND THE UNITED STATES

The third policy issue that is of vital importance for China is more complex, and its future evolution even more difficult to predict than that of the two mentioned above. However, it is here that Jews could make a real impact, and where they could formulate specific and compelling Jewish policy options. China's multi-faceted interdependence with the United States is larger than both countries sometimes wish to admit. China needs the United States for its market (30 percent of all Chinese manufacturing exports go to the United States, its biggest single market), for access to its science and technology (42 percent of all Chinese students abroad are studying in the United States), for cooperative solutions to the problems of North Korea, Taiwan, Central Asia, and the Middle East, and more. The United States in turn needs China for a number of economic, trade, and financial reasons, and for cooperation in addressing the problems just mentioned, such as North Korea, etc. China is the United States' fastest growing export market, and has become indispensable to America's standard of living, although this is still barely recognized by the American public. No other country or group of countries could presently manufacture at equally low prices the broad range and huge quantity of goods that

China ships to the United States, from daily consumer products to sophisticated computer components. Economic interdependence, the security of Middle Eastern oil supplies, Islamic militancy, and the threat of terrorism will compel China and the United States to continue seeking common ground, as they have been doing since 11 September 2001. However, this trend could also be severely disturbed by sudden events in Taiwan, Korea, or China itself.

American politicians and experts are conducting a lively public debate on future relations between China and the United States, with widely varying predictions. Some still see in China mainly a Communist dictatorship posing long-term strategic and economic threats to the United States. Using traditional models of power politics, they perceive a major military conflict between the two countries as ultimately inevitable. A mirror image of this pessimistic view can be found in China as well (Chapter 9.1), and the two parallel views probably keep reinforcing each other. Others, on the other hand, argue that this type of traditional geopolitical thinking is outmoded in today's world. They assert that globalization has altered the old rules of the game in power politics, and that an increasingly cooperative relationship between China and the United States is much more likely than the opposite. A China expert at Massachusetts Institute of Technology (MIT) defends the second argument by pointing to China's dependence on foreign technology and to

> the strategic benefits the United States is reaping from the particular way in which China has joined the global economy ... The United States and China are developing precisely the type of economic relationship that U.S. strategy has long sought to create ... As an open economy and a large importing country, China could be an ally of the United States in many areas of global trade and finance.[31]

American Jewish politicians and experts participate in these discussions as Americans — not as hypothetical supporters of Jewish causes. In general, the traditional political attitudes of most American Jews have been internationalist rather than isolationist, aimed at cooperation between countries, not confrontation. Many Jewish leaders recognize the long-term strategic importance of China, but pay little attention to the complex and sometimes tense triangular relationship that links Washington, Beijing, and Jerusalem. American Jewish interest in China has several sources. One is concern for Israel and interest in China's position on the Middle East. To this can be added an interest in the history of Jews in China in old times and in Shanghai in the twentieth century, sympathy with China's struggles, particularly during World War II, and appreciation of the historical absence of hostility to Jews in China.

Jews should have a strong incentive to act for better relations between the United States and China, and against the emergence of new tensions. This incentive, however, must remain subject to their concern for the interests of their own particular country of citizenship. The issue of Israel cannot be ignored in this context. Twice already, Chinese-American tensions have exacted a heavy price from Israel. Israel's efforts to establish normal relations with a not-yet-hostile, new China were nipped in the bud by the Korean War of 1950-53, which also helped to usher in a period of Chinese hostility to the Jewish state and support for Arab extremism that lasted one generation. In 2000, when the United States government forced Israel to cancel a legally binding contract to build two reconnaissance planes for China (the "Falcon Affair"), it severely damaged the new trust that the two countries had patiently built in each other over more than twenty years, since China began to abandon its active hostility. China and Israel agreed in 2003 to "open a new book" in their relations, but the scars are still visible and the "affair" continues to reverberate.

American Jews have a number of assets in dealing with China:

- The widespread Chinese awareness of the influence and power of the American Jewish community.
- The interest that leaders of Jewish organizations have in China and their sympathy for it. The American Jewish Committee (AJC) particularly maintains a continuous dialogue with China's leaders and visits China regularly.
- American Jewish sinologists. The Chinese know that Jews have been influential interpreters of their country's history and culture in the West (see Historic Appendix, section 4).
- A professional-academic organization dedicated to the enhancement of links between Chinese and Jews, the *Sino-Judaic Institute* in Menlo Park, California.[32]

What then could and should American Jews do in regard to China? As the American Jewish community is one of the two main pillars of a Jewish people policy towards China, its options and contributions are discussed in Chapters 8.4 and 9.1. There are, however, issues on which American Jews should act alone and inside the United States. First, American Jews should pay more attention to the triangular relationship between the United States, China, and Israel. This does not and must not contradict obvious and overriding national interests of the United States. Second, China and the Chinese American community are concerned that American perceptions of the Chinese are distorted and prejudiced. They estimate that 80 percent, if not more, of the United States Congress have negative views of China, reflecting public opinion. Research in 2001 has shown that prejudices against China and Chinese American citizens are closely linked, and that some "anti-Chineseness" is often expressed in terms that are almost identical to present and past "anti-Jewishness."[33] Two thirds of all Americans follow the pessimistic geopolitical view of China and consider China a future threat to the United States (this research was carried out before 11 September 2001; results might be different today). One third believes that Chinese Americans are more loyal to China than to the United States. Important American stereotypes are that Chinese Americans have too much power and influence and that they are clannish and dishonest in business. American Jews have been victims of similar stereotypes. Chinese American associations have established contact with Jewish American associations to explore common experiences and approaches. It would behoove American Jews to help American Chinese in the fight against the type of prejudice from which they have suffered for so long themselves, and which indirectly, may add to the tensions in the relations between China and the United States.

The American Jewish community is undoubtedly the strongest and most influential of all Jewish communities outside Israel. This does not mean that other Jewish communities could or should not play a bigger role in strengthening the links between China and the Jewish people. Jewish institutions in the United Kingdom have already shown growing interest in Sino-Judaic studies and links, and the Jews of Russia, China's large neighbor, should show greater interest in China as well. The European continent and Australia have dynamic Jewish communities. They may not be as influential as America's Jews, but they do have many academic and business links with China that could contribute to an enhancement of Chinese-Jewish relations.

4. THE EVOLUTION OF CHINA'S RELATIONS WITH ISRAEL

The state-to-state relations between China and Israel are not a theme of this report, but they are closely related to its main theme, considering that almost half of the Jewish people are living in Israel. The preceding discussion of three Chinese policy challenges of relevance to the Jewish people has shown that each of them is, or could become connected with an "Israel factor." This applies particularly to the relationship between American Jews and China, but Israel is directly or indirectly, willingly or unwillingly, also present in China's concerns about its oil supply and its Moslems. China's relations with Israel are of old standing and preceded the establishment of official diplomatic relations (1991) by more than a decade. It has been widely reported that the first relations between the two countries were in the military as well as agricultural sectors, with China showing great appreciation for Israel's technological edge in both. Relations are continuing in various fields of technology, as they are in academic and cultural fields, in spite of the severe setback caused by the "Falcon Affair." Israel can count on friends in China's defense, agriculture, and academic establishments, among others. It is interesting that Israel's technological contributions to China in the military and agricultural sectors seem to be known and popular widely beyond the leadership circles. These contributions can come up in discussions with students in the cities, or with simple farmers in the countryside who seem to know more about Israel's agro-technical achievements than farmers in the West. On the political and diplomatic levels, relations were good until the "Falcon Affair" and the beginning of the Intifada. They have deteriorated sharply since, but now seem to be improving, as illustrated by the state visit to China of Israel's President Katzav in December 2003.

Chinese government circles are not necessarily of one opinion about Israel; there seem to be positive and negative trends. This huge and complex country does not always speak with one voice, and there are gaps between what officials say in public and private. Public statements on the Arab-Israeli conflict have always given generous support to the Arab and particularly Palestinian side, and so have China's votes in the United Nations, without damaging China's pragmatic relations with Israel. However, a prominent and one-sided presentation of the Intifada by the Chinese media has damaged

Israel's public reputation, and if it continues, might also affect that of the Jewish people as a whole. Chapter 7.3 discusses the challenge that this situation raises for a Jewish people policy.

Providing policy advice to Jewish policy makers in this complex situation is not an easy task. Certainly, the fact that many Chinese are curious and willing to learn about Israel and the Jews (Chapters 4, 5, and 6) underscores the need for long-term cultural policies among others, as advocated in this report. But it might also be necessary to define more clearly both the differences and links between Israeli state and Jewish people policy in regard to China. Israeli state policy and Jewish people policy are not one and the same, and in many respects, will remain independent of each other. Some components of the Sino-Israeli relationship cannot be Jewish people policy concerns. However, in other respects, particularly when there is a real danger to Jews anywhere in the world or when the standing of the Jewish people as a whole is affected, Israeli state and Jewish people policy must become closely linked, if not identical.

In examining the relations between China and Israel and how they are connected to other factors — oil, the Moslem world, and US policies — two additional comments must be made. First, relations between China and Israel can have many cross-country effects because so many other countries are watching China's increasing economic and geopolitical weight and want to position themselves with regard to the changing global power constellations. The inverse is true as well: China will watch Israel's foreign relations; its interest in the evolution of Indian-Israeli relations has been mentioned above. Of course, India is likely to follow the development of Sino-Israeli links with equal attention. And the same is likely to hold true for many other countries that have important relations with China, Israel, or both: Japan, Korea, the Southeast Asian countries, Russia, Turkey, European countries. The Sino-Israeli relationship could have indirect repercussions beyond the direct mutual interests of both countries.

Second, China's concern about Middle Eastern stability or instability has already been mentioned (Chapter 3.1). Chinese policy makers and advisors are considering how China could contribute to stability; there have been discussions between Chinese experts on whether or not China should join the Middle Eastern peace "Quartet" as an independent actor (thereby forming a "Quintet"). Some have recommended such a move to the Chinese government, others are opposed to it. Israel might want to reflect on how China could be involved in Middle Eastern peacemaking. The likely positive or negative effects of any move must be carefully evaluated before a specific proposal is made, but it is not too early for Israel to begin thinking about possible future options. In any event, Chinese policy experts are already thinking about them.

4. Beginning Chinese Awareness of the Jewish People

1. JEWISH ENCOUNTERS WITH CHINA: A SUMMARY

Before discussing the beginning of Chinese knowledge of the Jews, a short note is necessary on Jewish knowledge of China, although the emphasis of this report is on the former rather than the latter theme. It is both a Jewish and Chinese tradition to continuously recall old history, to refer to precedents of past centuries in order to build "a bridge across broken time."[34] Jewish policy makers should keep in mind that there is a history of past encounters between Chinese and Jews that is too little known, or better, a history of meetings between their cultures, a history of mutual awareness. Sino-Jewish encounters were coincidental, often interrupted by distance and historic catastrophes, but never hostile. Until the twentieth century, these encounters had no influence on the fate of either people. Modern Jewish interest in China emerged in the late nineteenth century and continued through the twentieth century. This is a little explored field. The Jewish interest often indicated sympathy for China and its people and suffering, respect for its philosophy, culture, and art, and also recognition that in China, Jews have never been ill treated. (For a more extensive historic summary see Historic Appendix).

Jewish interest in China shows awareness of a larger context in which Jews and Judaism could exist, far beyond the familiar Ancient World, Christian, or Moslem environments. Jews have been ready to look beyond themselves, linking themselves as Jews to one of the most remote cultural environments. Thus, there is a good historic basis for improving the links between Chinese and Jews, beyond the dictates of "realpolitik." Israel's founding father and first prime minister, David Ben-Gurion, was deeply convinced that Chinese and Jews had something to say to each other. During the early 1950s, Ben-Gurion tried assiduously to establish diplomatic relations with the People's Republic of China. His concern went beyond "realpolitik." On several occasions he exhorted Israel and the Jews to look to China (and India); it was important for the Jewish people to seek spiritual and cultural relations with Asia's great, old civilizations. It remains a challenge to Jewish policy makers of the twenty-first century to listen to his call.

2. AWARENESS OF THE JEWISH PEOPLE IN NINETEENTH- AND EARLY TWENTIETH-CENTURY CHINA

Chinese awareness of Jews in modern times first emerged in the 1830s and 1840s, in the wake of Protestant missionary teachings and Bible translations. The "Jew," however defined, became a subject of intellectual and political debate. Some intellectual and political consequences of the Protestant "import" from the West became clear soon enough: the leaders of the Taiping Rebellion, which devastated China between 1851 and 1864 and tried to overthrow the ruling dynasty, attacked the "Jews" because they had rejected the Christian Savior — a trace of the Taiping's earlier missionary contacts.

In the second half of the century, real, contemporary Jews entered the Chinese conscience. A first sketch of Jewish history, which was still seen as a chapter of Christian history, dates back to 1850 (Xu Jiyu). Also early Chinese traveler-scholars visited the West and mentioned the Jews. Some of the still-dominant Chinese stereotypes of Jews began to take form: Jews are rich and talented, particularly in business, and some of them are dishonest (the reproach made by the Taiping). They are seen to have enormous power in America, financial and other (noted already in 1903!).

Only towards the end of the nineteenth and in the first two decades of the twentieth century did Chinese historians discover the Jews of Kaifeng. Initially, these Jews were considered to be no more than one of China's numerous exotic sects. No link was made between them and the earlier Chinese writings about the Jews of the world and their fate. A certain reluctance to link the two has remained, partly because interest in the Jews of Kaifeng is not encouraged by the Chinese authorities (Chapter 8.2).[35]

The surprised Chinese travelers of the nineteenth century also reported that Jews were often discriminated in the West and persecuted by pogroms in Russia. The Jew as victim of the "white man" remained an image of enduring power in the Chinese conscience, strongly reinforced after the *Shoah*. Thus, the image of the Jew also became linked to internal Chinese struggles and fears. Statements that may sound anti-Jewish to Western ears often relate to these struggles. Of Shakespeare's plays, none was more frequently translated into Chinese than *The Merchant of Venice*. It helped establish the image of the moneygrabbing Jew, but also of the Jew who rebels against Western persecution and humiliation. This second image introduced the Jew as a "brother" of the suffering, exploited Chinese. It is this image of Shylock that was propagated by Chinese nationalists and left-wing intellectuals.

For those Chinese who saw a parallel between the fate of the Jews and their own, the balance between negative and positive stereotypes began to swing towards the latter. Chinese newspapers vehemently reproached Czarist Russia for the infamous pogrom of Kishinev in 1903, where many Jews were killed and injured. They compared this massacre to preceding Russian brutalities where many Chinese had been slaughtered. The tragedy of the stateless Jewish people became a metaphoric warning to the Chinese, who at the turn of the century saw their own country collapse. "The past of the Jews is China's today, the present of the Jews will be the future of China,"[36] feared a patriotic writer.

The poet Chen Tianhua lamented in 1903, "I pity the Jew who scurries about, without a home to which to return." The leading reformist Kang Youwei — who in 1898 had told the young Emperor Guang Xu face to face that China's legal, political, and social system had to be radically changed — wrote in 1909 about the Jews: "They have a family but not a country, everywhere they are cast into abuse and difficulty."[37] It was thus no surprise that some Chinese intellectuals supported Zionism as the best solution to Jewish homelessness. The approval of one of these intellectuals had weighty political consequences. It was that of Sun Yatsen, the greatly respected founder and first president of the Chinese Republic. For him, the connection between old Jewish history, modern Jewish tragedy, and the Zionist program was compelling, and so was the similarity between the fate of the Jews and the Chinese. He compared the two peoples in surprising terms, almost identical to those used by Spinoza, 250 years before.[38]

Chinese nationalism disappeared when China was conquered by foreigners [the Manchus]. But China was not the only nation that had been conquered. The Jewish people also lost their country ... Though their country was destroyed, the Jewish nation has existed to this day ... [Zionism] is one of the greatest movements of the present time. All lovers of democracy cannot help but support whole-heartedly ... the movement to restore your wonderful and historical nation, which has contributed so much to the civilization of the world and which rightly deserves an honorable place in the family of nations.[39]

Debates on the Jewish people went on from the 1920s to the 1940s, again closely related to China's own internal struggles. Not all supported Zionism — some attacked it as imperialist and capitalist. Jews interested the Chinese reformers and modernizing elites, but some of them, belonging to the May Fourth reform movement that started after 1918, rejected Judaism as old and superstitious, to be discarded exactly like Confucianism. In the late 1920s, European anti-Semitism started to seep into China; the *Protocols of the Elders of Zion* appeared in Chinese at this time. After the outbreak of the Sino-Japanese War in 1937, Chinese newspapers began to translate and publish distinctly anti-Semitic articles by Japanese authors that emphasized the alleged danger of Jewish financial power.[40] Again, these foreign imports found their way into the political discourse, as they did in the time of the Taiping. Some of Chiang Kaishek's associates, including his wife (who wanted to please her anti-Semitic friends in American high society), were heard to express anti-Semitic opinions. Today, few or no echoes seem to remain of these old debates.

During the same decades, Jewish culture affected Chinese culture directly, and perhaps for the first time in major ways. The reception of Yiddish writers in China — more than forty Yiddish short stories were translated into Chinese from the 1920s on — reinforced heated discussions about the need for language reform. The language reformers presented Yiddish, the language of simple people that had become the language of great literature as well, as an example to be emulated by China. This was apparently an attractive concept, as the classical Chinese language could no longer be spoken, read, or understood by the people.

Equally important was the enormous influence that the Jewish Bible had on Chinese fiction and letters between the 1920s and 1940s. Chinese intellectuals read the Bible as poetry, compared it to antique Chinese texts, and praised its literary value or drew parallels between the destruction of the Jewish and Chinese nations. When Mao Dun, one of the greatest Chinese writers of the century, fled before the Japanese occupiers, he quoted the dire predictions of the prophet Isaiah for the people of Israel as applying to China as well. In one of his most famous works, *Samson's Revenge* of 1942, Israel's biblical hero, who brings the temple crashing down on his foreign torturers, becomes a symbol of China's suffering under foreign occupation. The Bible found its way into the stories of many other Chinese writers, and the Chinese Bible text had a distinct influence on Chinese language and colloquial literature.

But interest in the Jewish Bible was not limited to its literary value. Already in the nineteenth century, a scholar (Liu Changxing, 1876) looked for affinities between the Ten Commandments and Confucian ethics. Lin Yutang, the prestigious Chinese writer, went further. In his preface to a new edition of Confucius's *Analects* he wrote in 1938:

> The body of Confucian thought resembles most the laws of Moses, and it is easier to compare Confucius in the scope of his teachings to Moses than to any other philosopher. The "li" of Confucius, like the law of Moses, covers both religious laws and laws of civil life … The "religion of li", like Judaism, embraces both religious worship and daily life, down to the matter of eating and drinking.[41]

This sounds like an echo back through the centuries, a late Chinese response to the words that the Jews of Kaifeng had incised on their stone monument of 1489: "The Confucian religion and this religion … agree on essential points and differ in secondary ones." Only now the tables were turned. In 1489, the highest standard of culture in Chinese eyes was Confucianism, to which the Jews wished to adapt. In 1938, the old Chinese certainty of cultural superiority had collapsed. The standard was now Western, and Lin Yutang, who wanted to improve the standing of Chinese culture in Western eyes at a time when China was in turmoil, used (in 1938!) Judaism as the high standard, because his Christian education had taught him to consider it as the basis of Western civilization.

After the foundation of the People's Republic of China in 1949, the Bible lost its prominent place in China's literary and political discourse for the following twenty years, and from the late 1950s on, Jewish studies could not be taught or even publicly mentioned. But the influence of Jewish letters emerged again, first with translations of the great American Jewish writers of the postwar period (Saul Bellow, Isaac Bashevis Singer). These translations became possible after the Cultural Revolution and before Israeli books could be published. The establishment of diplomatic relations with Israel in 1991 was followed by an increasing number of translations of Hebrew poetry and literature.

A special chapter in the more recent development of Chinese awareness of the Jewish people is the history of the Jewish refugee communities in Harbin and Shanghai before and during World War II. Both communities have left their mark on their cities, and their cultural contributions, e.g., to music, have been researched and documented. Several Chinese born in Shanghai who later reached senior positions in their country, had heard of, or met, Jews for the first time in their city of origin. Over the last few years, a growing number of Chinese voices were calling for protection of the country's cultural heritage against the radical urban development plans that were transforming all Chinese cities into more or less identical replicas of some modern Western models. This general cultural concern is now coinciding with renewed Chinese and Jewish interest in the Jewish past of Shanghai and Harbin. The Academies of Social Sciences in both cities, as well as other provincial and municipal authorities, have begun to pay attention to the cultural and tourist value of the former Jewish buildings and other sights. They are encouraging the restoration and preservation not only of some of the buildings themselves, but also of the historic memory attached to them. Books, seminars, research projects, and commemorative events all serve this purpose. Foreign Jews, particularly former residents of Shanghai and Harbin, participate in these efforts and help to raise money.[42] Permanent, visual monuments are certainly an effective method of preserving the memory of historic links between China and the Jews. Hopefully, this will not detract from other, no less important methods and goals of cultural outreach.

5. Present Judaic Scholarship and its Influence

1. A NARROW ACADEMIC BASE WITH A BROAD OUTREACH

The number of Chinese experts and scholars specializing in Jewish and Israeli history and culture or in the Hebrew language, is still small for a great power of more than 1,340 million inhabitants. However, according to many, their work over the last twenty years has had a broad and positive effect in China.

China has today between eight and ten known and relatively active academic centers for Jewish and Israeli studies, of greatly varying size. There are also a few centers that had or have again some interest in these topics but are currently less active. Fewer than twenty Chinese scholars (perhaps fifteen) devote themselves full-time to Judaic studies, alongside thirty to forty graduate students (M.A.s and Ph.D.s). There are maybe up to two hundred scholars who are involved in Jewish studies on a part-time basis, and a larger number of undergraduate students. Three universities (Shanghai, Nanjing, and Kaifeng) can grant degrees in Jewish history and culture, and another (Jinan) in Jewish philosophy. The North-Western University in Xi'an and the Foreign Studies University of Shanghai can grant degrees in Middle Eastern studies.

The creation of scholarly groups in research institutions and universities is a welcome development of the last twenty-five years. It replaced the isolated, individual Judaic scholars of earlier times. The largest Judaica library in China, and probably the largest on the Asian continent outside Israel, is at the University of Nanjing, with 7,000 books. There are smaller libraries in other academic institutions that are often difficult to access, and a small library and reading room in the Israeli Embassy.

The University of Beijing has a modern Hebrew language class (in the Western Languages Department of the School of Foreign Languages), where twelve students follow a four-year course. By 2003, thirty Chinese students had graduated this course. In Shanghai and other universities, there are shorter courses of basic Hebrew. A much larger number of Chinese are learning biblical Hebrew (approximately one hundred); these are students of the Nanjing Union Theological Seminary — a teacher-training college for future Protestant priests. In all of China, there are probably two or three Chinese who are proficient in biblical Hebrew, and a few more in Israel.

The output of these scholars can be measured against the number of Chinese publications per year. China publishes 30-40,000 new books annually, including translations (for France, the figure for 2002 was 43,000). Of these, the overwhelming majority are professional, fictional, or other "recreational" genres, and only 1,000-1,500 are serious books about history and foreign countries or cultures. Of these, between 10 and 20 are published every year on Jewish or Israeli subjects, including translations, with the number slowly increasing. In most cases, 3,000 or 5,000 copies are printed, in exceptional cases there are 10,000 or second prints. (These figures are typical for most specialized, scholarly books in China.) Since the early 1980s, when books on Jewish themes appeared again in China, 200-300 such titles have been printed, many of them serious, others more popular or sensational. Chinese scholars consider these numbers as relatively high in comparison to many other cultures. When Judaic studies became possible again after the Cultural Revolution, Chinese scholars had to start from scratch. They began with translations of Western books on Israel and Jewish history, and continued with new Chinese books on the same subjects, and on Israel's political structure, foreign relations, and economic and agricultural performance. A theme of predilection from then until today is Israel's Mossad — more than ten books on the Mossad's exploits have been written or translated and all found avid Chinese readers. Books on Jewish culture and religion followed later because these subjects were intellectually more difficult than Jewish history for Chinese readers with no religious experience whatsoever. Recent publications include books on Jewish history from Abraham to the State of Israel, or specific periods, such as the ancient Jewish kingdom, the modernization of Judaism in the eighteenth century, the *Shoah*, the hunt for Nazi criminals, the birth and growth of Israel, the Arab-Israeli conflict, as well as on Jewish philosophy, literature, and religion. The years after 1995 saw a growing number of translations of sophisticated Jewish philosophical and religious texts of old and modern times, including Moses Maimonides' *Guide of the Perplexed* (*More Nevukhim*), and the rabbinic and Talmudic texts *Sayings of the Fathers* (*Pirquei Avoth*) and *Derekh Eretz Suta*, with its appendix *Chapter on Peace* (*Perekh ha-Shalom*), published in 2003. In general, one can say that there has been a shift from the general introductions of earlier times to more monographic works.

However, few Chinese authors limit themselves to one period or aspect of Jewish history. Most of the main authors have written, for example, on old Jewish and new Israeli history or culture, on Jewish religion and the Israeli economy, on the Arab-Israeli conflict, and on the history of Moslems and Jews in China under the Song and Yuan Dynasties centuries ago. This diversity can be both a strength and a weakness. A strength when it reflects a Chinese tradition of explaining current events by looking at history, but also a weakness when it stems from a lack of depth and originality. It may be due to an inability to read sources in their original language, or a lack of interest by publishers and audiences that are not looking for in-depth analyses but quick and easy information, or other university duties that may impose limits on scholarly specialization. Reviewing the Chinese authors of Judaic and Israeli studies between 1980 and today, one finds a number of names of the 1980s and early 1990s that have since disappeared. Except for a few, there is not yet a strong and stable

Judaic scholarship community with a long-term commitment (or with long-term academic employment, which is perhaps one of the main problems).

In the years since 2000, the Intifada has created additional problems for Judaic scholarship. The Israeli-Palestinian conflict seems to be a burden on some of the intellectuals who had chosen the Jews and Israel as research themes ten or fifteen years ago, when both were popular. They may ask themselves now whether these are still the most promising subjects for their own standing and career in China. This can lead to expressions of anger at Israel or its present policies. It is important for the Jewish people to avoid over-reliance on a limited circle of old friends, and seek to enlarge it by new friends.

In 1992, one of China's foremost Judaic experts passed critical judgment on his country's scholarship:

> Compared to the advanced level of studies internationally, however, we still have a long way to go in developing the range and depth of our research ... The continuing study of China's Jewish community is the sole area where Chinese scholars of Jewish studies can pride themselves on having reached an international level.[43]

However, these sober words must not blind one to the merits of China's Judaic scholars, nor obscure the fact that they were struggling with difficulties that few other Judaic scholars in the world had to face in the twentieth century. These scholars were born into one of the oldest still-living civilizations, which was until the nineteenth century not influenced by the other, almost equally old culture of the Jews. They had no Jewish family background, generally had not known Jews in their youth, and had few, if any, personal connections with Judaism, Christianity, or Islam. They lived through one of their country's most radical revolutions, during which the study of Jewish topics was unthinkable. When they emerged in widely separate parts of China, they "discovered" the Jews, each at a different occasion and with different motives. For some, Jewish studies were a passing fad or at best a novelty that might enhance their university careers; for others it became a true intellectual commitment. These Judaic scholars still lack the language skills to do original research by today's exacting criteria (similar to much European Judaic scholarship until the nineteenth century), but they bring to the table a unique ability to look at Jews with eyes not trained in — or blurred by — Christian, Islamic, anti-Semitic, or European Communist traditions. Their books and articles cannot be easily evaluated internationally because, apart from some excerpts, none has been translated from Chinese into other languages. Many are likely to recycle Western material, but some might provide new insights into Jewish history from the perspectives of Chinese history. Jews can learn something from China's views. Jews have an interest in becoming acquainted with China's unique, unfettered perspectives, particularly when these are part of comparative studies that show parallels with Chinese literature, legends, and history. There is at least one respected Jewish thinker who has understood this: Rabbi Adin Steinsaltz of Jerusalem. He commented on the great scholarly interest in Jews that he encountered during his visit to China:

The problem is, that what they found in Judaism, most Jews don't see. We need to bring them back to our traditions, so that they can be proud again.[44]

Some Chinese insights are simple but striking. The great writer Mao Dun depicts the crucifixion of Jesus as a "politically motivated murder of a prisoner of conscience."[45] This is not such a far-fetched interpretation for a Chinese who lived through the bloodshed and political murders of the Guomindang period and the Japanese occupation, and who noted the similarity with the conditions of Judaea in the first century C.E. However, this is not a comment one would expect from a Western Christian writer.

Original judgments can be found in the writings of young students who look at Jews without prejudice. The following statements were written verbatim in English, by students of the Beijing Foreign Studies University (BFSU) who replied at the end of 2003 to a questionnaire about Jews and Judaism. Annex 3 summarizes this survey.[46] These statements are not representative in a strict statistical sense, but they illustrate opinion trends that have already been noted by Chinese and Jewish observers, and are also reflected in books and articles. The students responded to a question asking what they know about Jewish history or culture:

A: I think Jewish people have a different way of thinking. I think they do have a closest relationship with God as God was invented by them (it is not a joke).
B: Jews have a long history of being persecuted. They have a strong sense of family and friends. They believe they're chosen by the God so they don't convert others.
C: In history, the Jewish people were repressed time and again, as a result, they scattered around the world ... They cherish knowledge greatly because knowledge is the only thing that can not be arrested away by others ...

It is not easy to assess the outreach of Judaic studies in China. How many people have really read any of the books and articles printed and sold in the last twenty years? Did books influence the elites and decision makers? Of 214 BFSU students who responded to the questionnaire mentioned above, 145 said that they got their knowledge on Jews from books, and twenty more from the Bible. Even considering that students are requested to read books, the figure of 145 is high because Jewish studies were not part of these students' curriculum. China remains a book-reading country. But published books alone cannot measure the actual output of China's Judaic scholars. These few scholars have over the years taught thousands of young Chinese, helped to organize exhibitions that attracted tens of thousands of visitors, some have spoken on Chinese television to millions of viewers, and a few have provided discreet advice to critical opinion makers and government leaders. Their impact must not be underestimated.

2. WHO IS ADVISING THE LEADERS OF CHINA?

All think tanks and policy advisors grapple with the same basic questions, whatever the country: Do policy makers want advice? Do they listen to advice? Whose advice? How to become an advisor? How to influence the decision makers? Chinese answers to these questions would be helpful in assessing whether China's Judaic scholarship could influence the country's leaders.

The question of who are the advisors was most easy to answer in Mao Zedong's time: he was China's chief "advisor" himself and destroyed the intellectual class, which for hundreds of years had "advised" and ruled China. Part of the reason for their persecution was the traditional Chinese view of intellectuals as the nation's teachers, perpetuating a culture that was to be abolished. Mao's successor, Deng Xiaoping, who had to cope with the consequences of the Cultural Revolution, created the Chinese Academy of Social Sciences (CASS) in Beijing in 1977. CASS and its many institutes functioned as the main advisory body for China's Central Government and Communist Party, with a president who for a long time was a senior member of the Government and the Party. Under the presidency of Deng's successor, Jiang Zemin, little seemed to change in the status and function of CASS. In fact, both Deng Xiaoping and Jiang Zemin shared the same view that intellectuals were essential to China's becoming rich and powerful again because they were holding the keys to science, technology, and most other foundations of a modern economy. Nevertheless, the old, close, and subservient relationship between the Chinese intellectuals and the state seemed to be broken, or at least radically transformed.[47]

Since 2001, when President Hu Jintao took over many of President Jiang Zemin's functions, observers felt that changes were in the air. One change, on which everybody seems to agree, is that the new president, a university graduate (as was already Jiang Zemin), will expose himself to external professional and technical advice more willingly and frequently than his revolutionary predecessors, and that this will be true of his government in general. Both Chinese and foreign observers have noted President Hu Jintao's eagerness to meet with intellectuals, and reported that he has instituted regular consultations with some of the country's leading thinkers on a wide variety of Chinese and global issues.[48] Probably not unrelated to this, a quiet but potentially significant modification in China's leadership occurred in 2002, when five of the seven members of the Politburo of the Communist Party, and more than half of the two hundred members of the Central Committee stepped down, and all of them were replaced by university graduates.[49] These are drastic changes indeed, compared to the late 1970s when almost none of the Party leaders had university education.

A third change, on which there is not yet general agreement, relates to the identification of the main advisory bodies. There is an impression that CASS, while still associated with and trusted by the government, is no longer exactly what it used to be, and that a few elite universities, particularly Beijing's BEIDA and RENMIN[50] universities, have begun to take over some of its functions. Other academic centers, particularly in Shanghai, might also be mentioned in this context. The two universities in Beijing would like to build up their competence in Middle Eastern studies among others, but have financial constraints or difficulties in finding top quality specialists. At the same time, the CASS Institute of World Religions has indicated the wish to set up a Jewish study center, which would be the first in CASS, and is looking for Jewish partners. Members of CASS assert that they continue to be "the government" and deny that they are losing ground. But their competitors affirm the contrary with equal conviction. CASS may be vulnerable: its Achilles' heel is perhaps that it plays no role in higher education. Chinese television seems to anticipate subtle shifts in power: its main political commentators are more often than in the past, chosen from the universities rather than CASS.

Many consider the Ministry of Foreign Affairs' Research Center as the government's main source of information on global issues. It is often regarded as a most professional and experienced source. How well connected is it to Chinese academia? Academic experts complain in China, as they do in all countries, that the government is not paying enough attention to their advice. In order to increase their impact on government policy, several groups studying Middle Eastern, Jewish, and other related issues have agreed to cooperate by organizing closed conferences that the government is invited to attend. The subjects include the Arab-Israeli conflict, World Jewry, the Iraq conflict, and how to involve China in the Middle East. Government delegates come from the West Asia Department of the Foreign Ministry and from the research center of China's State Council (Cabinet). Nobody can say whether senior policy makers read the summaries written after these conferences, and whether they have an impact. However, China's top leaders do at least occasionally read published scholarly articles on Middle Eastern issues directly touching on their country's interests. One indication of this is that the author of one such article from an important provincial university received personal congratulations in 2003 from one of China's Cabinet members. Jewish policy makers will need to ask for the advice of the Chinese government to understand the ongoing changes and find the appropriate partners for discussion and cooperation.

China presents a problem to Jews that does not exist in any other important, non-hostile country: that most of China's Judaic experts live and teach far away from the capital, which is the center of power. Beijing is the "weak link" that needs to be strengthened; the dilemma will be to identify the appropriate center for cooperation at a time when power seems to be shifting, and to do so without offending the important academic centers in Shanghai, which are also competing vigorously to keep their place as equivalent advisory bodies to the government in Beijing.

Are books important tools for influencing opinion leaders and policy makers? Again, opinions are divided. Some, who have written many books themselves, believe in their importance. Others have doubts whether and how much Chinese policy makers read, and some have even questioned how much their policy advisors do.

More direct ways are proposed to reach the ears of policy makers, such as restricted high-level seminars. While these are certainly most important, it is known that President Jiang Zemin for one has read books about Jews that have influenced his thought. In any event, senior Chinese scholars who know the United States well and have policy advisory roles in China are convinced that their own social status and influence on government policy is greater than that of their colleagues in America. Jewish policy makers would be well advised to pay attention to Chinese Judaic and Middle Eastern scholarship, simply because there are enough signs that China's leaders will increasingly listen to the expert advice of their scholars.

Current Chinese Views of Jews and Judaism

1. THE "JEW" IN CHINESE

The terms used by one nation or civilization for members of another are significant and consequential. The term for "Jew" in Chinese changed several times through the centuries. Chinese scholars are debating whether certain terms used for non-Chinese people in old chronicles mean Jews or something else. In all languages of the Christian and Moslem world, the word "Jew" carries heavy emotional and polemical baggage anchored in the founding texts of the two religions — the New Testament and the Koran. The Chinese terms do not carry this baggage. The first known and undisputed references to Jews in official Chinese documents appeared under the Yuan dynasty, when the Mongols ruled China (1279-1368). How did the Jews of Kaifeng call themselves? From the time of the Yuan on and during the following centuries, they called themselves "Israel," but did not use the word "Jew," as their Jesuit visitors reported with great interest.

The modern Chinese word for Jew, *youtai*, was introduced in the 1830s, probably by Protestant Bible translations where it seems to have appeared first. It could also have been derived from the almost identical Japanese term for Jew — the question is not settled. The Chinese character "you" has a radical referring to animals. This was used for all foreign ethnic groups, probably in a derogatory sense, but it also existed as an old Chinese family name. Some have suggested that *youtai* was originally meant to be derogatory, specifically for use in New Testament translations, but this has not been proven. If this character ever had a negative connotation in Chinese, it was lost long ago.

What is a Jew to the Chinese today? *Youtai* is used in various combinations:

Youtai jiao: the Jewish religion, cult, or sect

Jiao is the term used by nineteenth- and early twentieth-century Chinese historians for the Jews of Kaifeng: they were one of China's many "sects." Today, most Chinese are atheists. Religion is not much respected, and to be a member of a *jiao*, a religion or sect, confers no prestige in public opinion. Religions that have been practiced by substantial numbers of Chinese citizens for some time have received a kind of official recognition. They include Christianity and Islam. In addition, many numerically smaller native cults can be practiced without difficulty and do not require formal, official recognition, particularly if they are part of the culture of recognized national minorities. The term *jiao* is not used in relation to Chinese Jews today because there are none left by any currently agreed Jewish religious or Chinese administrative definition of Judaism.

Youtai minzu: the Jewish nationality or ethnicity

There are fifty-six recognized nationalities in China, but Jews are not among them. This situation is similar to that of other groups whose nationality status is not clear. In 1953, the Chinese authorities rejected a request by local authorities in the Henan province to grant Jewish descendents of Kaifeng nationality status. The reasons for this are given in Chapter 8.2. The term *minzu* would normally not be used for Jews in China, but could be used for Jewish minorities abroad. It has occasionally been translated as "race," which gives the term an unfortunate Western connotation that it does not carry in today's Chinese.

Youtai ren: the Jewish people, the Jews

This is the term most commonly used in daily language. It is a convenient term that has no negative connotation.

Youtai guo: the Jewish nation or state

This term is often used for the State of Israel, also *Israel guo*.

Youtai wenhua: the Jewish culture

Wenhua is a respectable term, but less comprehensive than *wenming*, "civilization," of which *wenhua* is only a part.

Youtai wenming: the Jewish civilization

Wenming is the most prestigious of all terms; *ming* means "radiance", "brightness". The Ming dynasty is the "Radiant Dynasty." Being called a "civilization" would put the Jews on a par with the Chinese who like to refer to themselves as *zhong hua* ("Middle Kingdom") *wenming*.

The Chinese don't have and never had a clear answer to the "Who is a Jew?" question, much less than the West. It is no coincidence then that there are Chinese books such as *Israel-The Mysterious Country* (Yang Menzu, 1992) or *Jews, a People of Mystery* (Xiao Xian, 2000). For this reason also, it is difficult in China to place the study of Judaism — the Jewish religion, nationality, people, nation, culture, civilization, or whatever — into the existing academic structures. In Nanjing, the Institute for Jewish Studies was, until 2003, part of the Institute of Foreign Literature because the founding director started as professor of modern American literature. But it has since been moved to the Institute of Religious Studies. In Kaifeng, in contrast, the Institute of Jewish Studies belongs to the College of History and Culture, but the same university also has a center for biblical Jewish literature that is part of the very prestigious Chinese Literature College. In Jinan, the Institute for Jewish Studies is part of the School of Philosophy, and in other academic and research institutes studies concerning Jews and Israel are located in the International Relations departments.

The book *Judaism as a Civilization* by Mordechai Kaplan, first published in 1934 in the United States, argues that it was a fatal mistake of the Enlightenment to present Judaism as a creed only and not as a culture or civilization that is expressing the full life of the Jewish people. This programmatic book was translated into Chinese in 1995 (University of Shandong in Jinan), using *wenming*, "civilization," in the title.

However, so far the location of Jewish study centers in China reflects less recognition of the notion of a Jewish civilization, than continuing confusion about this "mysterious" people — a confusion not unknown in the West and even among Jews themselves. In the late 1990s, a prominent Chinese expert wrote a memorandum to Chinese government agencies, arguing in favor of the recognition of Jews as an official religion. In 2000, the text appeared in English. This is how the author grappled with words to clarify the strange and often changing phenomenon of the Jews for China's officialdom:

> Because of the uniqueness of the history and culture of the Jewish people the nuances of the term Judaism are very broad. Its basic meaning is 'all Jews', but in fact it includes the whole of Jewish civilization. So the Jewish religion does not just mean the religious beliefs of the Jews, but also the visible shape of the culture of the Jewish people, and so it is frequently used to indicate generally Jewish culture or the kernel of Jewish culture. This is similar to the term Confucianism which in reality points to the heart of the Chinese culture. Further, in the course of a very long history, Jewish thought, spirit, religion, and culture — all aspects of the people were bound together and it would be very difficult to separate them.[51]

Since 2000, the Palestinian Intifada has added new questions to old problems of definition: Are Jews and Israelis the same? Are Israelis Jews? Does Israel represent all Jews? The "mystery" of the Jews is still not elucidated.

2. IMPORTANT CHINESE PERCEPTIONS

No opinion poll based on a statistically representative sample of the Chinese people on the perception of Jews has ever been conducted. This does not mean that there is nothing that can be said about the subject. This section uses the same four sources of information that are the basis for the entire report (see Annex 4): published literature, interviews with Chinese and Jewish experts, question-and-answer sessions with Chinese students (Annex 1), and the written survey of BFSU student perceptions already mentioned (Annex 3).

The four sources corroborate each other to a large degree, with some divergences that will be pointed out. The relative concordance cannot prove, but at least appears to support our conclusions and impressions. This is reassuring because the first two sources might be seen as somewhat biased: Jewish China experts may prefer to hear and report mainly the positive reactions to Jews, and China's Judaic scholars would quite naturally expect the subject of their academic endeavors to be generally attractive and popular. But the young students who attended the lectures on Jewish culture and the question-and-answer sessions, and those who participated in the BFSU survey spoke their mind with no visible inhibition. Their responses were in line with the other sources, but not obviously influenced by them. Much further study would be necessary to formulate a more scientific assessment of opinion trends, which could be done with the help of appropriate Chinese research bodies or through Internet polls, often used in China for commercial purposes.

The number of Chinese who have met, or

are aware of having met a Jew, is infinitesimally small in comparison with China's total population. Even the students of Jewish topics in Chinese universities have mostly never seen a Jew, except for rare foreign visitors. Only in China's governing elites and among intellectuals, scholars, businessmen, and technicians with foreign experience may one find a certain number of persons who have met Israeli, American, or other Jews. The general perceptions of Jews amongst the governing elites are little known, although some Chinese leaders have expressed friendly interest in Jews in the recent past.

It can safely be assumed that many of the current opinion trends about Jews have historic roots in prerevolutionary Chinese thought, as summarized in Chapter 4.2. Today's Chinese scholars sometimes refer back to significant, earlier statements, such as President Sun Yatsen's support for Zionism during the early 1920s. An important fact, often overlooked, is that in China, the Communist Revolution did not oppose or try to obliterate these earlier opinion trends. The personal attitude of China's Communist leaders to the Jewish people was radically different from that of the Soviet leaders and their European subordinates. Jews may have been of little importance to them, but a few documented statements and gestures, for example by Mao Zedong and Zhou Enlai,[52] indicate a measure of sympathy for Jews rather than antipathy. It is no wonder then that a small number of foreign Jews joined the Communists' fight against the Japanese occupants in the 1940s, befriended the revolutionary leaders, became Chinese citizens, and are being held in high esteem to this day. It is noteworthy that these Jews did not have to change their Jewish name or hide their origin, in stark contrast to East European and Soviet Communist practice. Later on, during the 1960s and 1970s, Zionism was denounced as an ally of American imperialism, etc., but this was never linked to Soviet-style anti-Semitism.

Most of the Chinese concepts about Jews that are found in the four sources of this report, can be grouped under four headings:

- Jewish wealth, success, and power, including more recently, military success
- Jewish contributions to world civilization, particularly in science and technology, and their link to Jewish modernization
- the longevity of the Jewish people
- the persecution of Jews through the ages, particularly during the *Shoah*

Among a minority, a new, negative stereotype may be in the process of formation: Jews as "aggressors" and "killers" of the weak and innocent. Time will tell whether this new stereotype is a passing phenomenon, or could become more permanent among a part of the public and the politically interested elites unless there is a suitable Jewish information policy.

There are other important characteristics of Jewish culture and faith that do not get Chinese attention. One subject that does not attract great interest beyond a few Judaic scholars is Jewish ethics, personal and social. What exactly are the values and norms that Jews have been fighting and dying for over thousands of years, and have these values any relevance for China? Apparently no major books have been written and few students have asked questions about some of the main moral values of Judaism from the earliest times on: the sanctity of human life, the religiously consecrated demands of impartial justice for all, the rights of the poor, and the duties of the rich. In line with China's main preoccupation of the day, Chinese interest is focused on the Jew as a model of worldliness and success.

Wealth and power

The image of Jewish riches has existed in China for more than a hundred years. Images of success and power are linked to it. The Jews are admired, but perhaps also envied because they are seen to have what every Chinese wants to have for himself and his nation: money, success, and power. Since the economic liberalization of the country and in the wake of rapid economic growth, many Chinese have become obsessed with the question of how to get rich, how to find a good job, and how to succeed in work, love, and any other endeavor. Mountains of popular books on success and wealth can be found on every street bookstall. Seminars on "how to succeed" are held in five- and four-star hotels in the big cities. Jews are identified with all three dreams. How to explain Jewish wealth and success? How to become a "Jew," or similar to a Jew? The explanations for Jewish money and the Jews' alleged dominance of business, the banks, the stock exchange, the world economy, etc., have varied. There have been a small number of anti-Semitic expressions in line with hostile European attitudes, particularly in biographical references to some of the former rich Jews of Shanghai. But in general, the Chinese traditions with regard to money and wealth are similar to those of the Jews, and different from the moral reticence that Christianity often maintained towards wealth.[53] Both Chinese and Jews celebrate riches, success, and well-being in this world, not poverty. Therefore, when Chinese authors speak admiringly of the "commercial consciousness" of the Jewish Bible, or "the special sense that Jews have about money," this must not be seen as a reflection of Western prejudice, though it may sound quite similar. It could mean something else that a foreigner would not immediately understand: one of the disguises a Chinese author may use to express his dislike of Communist egalitarianism. Equally, Jewish political and economic power in the West is often exaggerated as it is in Western anti-Semitic literature. However, this power is generally not presented as a threat, but as a reason for respect and envy, an achievement that the Chinese would like to emulate. But there are exceptions to this that are raised later.

A special case is the often outright Chinese admiration for Israel's military and intelligence capabilities and successes. Such admiration could be found in the West in the 1950s and 1960s, but has disappeared since. In China, it is reflected not only in books, but also on Chinese Internet sites.

Among students, there was a significant difference between those who had some prior interest in or knowledge of Jewish topics (Annexes 1 and 2), and those who did not (Annex 3). Hardly any of the former group repeated the usual clichés about Jewish wealth and business success, whereas a large number of students in the latter group did. To those students who had a real interest in Jewish tradition and history, wealth was apparently no longer the most noteworthy characteristic of the Jews.

Contributions to world civilization and modernization

Another Chinese cliché, almost as widespread as that about Jewish wealth, is that Jews have made great contributions to Western civilization. Again, admiration is mixed with some envy, but not hostility. The Jews are seen as contributors to religious, philosophical, and political ideas, and to economic and scientific progress that changed the world. Einstein is most often mentioned. When young Chinese are asked who their greatest twentieth-century hero is, they often reply, "Einstein." Other names are Marx, Freud, and Jesus. There are several Chinese books on famous Jews. One, *The Biographies of the Famous Jewish Intellectuals* (1995), is written in popular style and contains more than ninety biographies of three or four pages each. This book might help us to better understand some Chinese idiosyncrasies, although it would be dangerous to generalize on the basis of a single publication. The earliest Jew included is Spinoza, followed by Heine and Marx. The uninformed reader would not guess that there were Jews before the seventeenth century, or many important Jews before the twentieth century. What the reader will learn is that Jews are a quintessential part of twentieth-century history. Interestingly, the largest single group is of Jewish novelists and poets (twenty-three), followed by musicians and filmmakers (twelve), and painters (five). This is unusual; the BFSU students (all studying humanities, not science or technology) frequently referred to Jewish scientists, philosophers, and economists, but hardly ever to writers and artists. Seventeen scientists and mathematicians are included in the book, and six economists and other humanities scholars. Are there any Jewish statesmen worthy of mention? Only two: Leo Trotsky and Henry Kissinger. And finally (and this can be found in Western books as well), the reader is treated to a few erroneous "extras" — biographies of famous persons who are not Jews: Rainer Maria Rilke, Samuel Beckett, Pablo Picasso.

The question for the Chinese is, how could so few Jews contribute so much to the world, whereas the more numerous Chinese did not, at least not in modern times? What do the Jews have? Naturally, Chinese interest turns to Jewish education, as China has always attached great importance to learning. Do Jews owe their achievements to education? If so, which education? When students of Henan University in Kaifeng were asked in 2003 to freely choose any subject of Jewish history or culture and write a short paper about it, four of the thirty participants wrote papers with "Jewish education" or "Jewish science" in the title, and several of the subject matters chosen by the other twenty-six were related to education as well (Annex 2). Jewish education appears equally frequently in the responses of BFSU students (Annex 3). That Jews attach great value to education seems to be a widely shared impression amongst the Chinese.

It is no coincidence that the *Haskalah*, the history of the Jewish Enlightenment, is attracting the interest of some Judaic scholars who ask whether the secret source of the Jewish contribution to modernity lies in this period. The Jewish Enlightenment started in the second part of the eighteenth century, but the fight between the Old and the New is still going on and the debate has never been resolved. There was no quick revolutionary resolution of this debate as there was in China, when the proclamation of the People's Republic in 1949 led to a radical destruction of old values, beliefs, and structures. But how then did the Jews modernize? How does their modernization compare to that of the Chinese? Was their modernization identical with Westernization? These are also core questions of contemporary Chinese history. In 2003, China's main academic journal of world religions published an article on Moses Mendelssohn by a Judaic scholar, and the same author published simultaneously a book on the Jewish Enlightenment.[54] Another scholar commented and translated into Chinese a number of classical Jewish texts by modern post-Enlightenment authors, such as Martin Buber, Leo Baeck, Cecil Roth and Mordechai Kaplan.[55] The questions of these Chinese scholars about the relationship between the old and the new in Jewish culture, seem to echo the questions that Jewish sinologists had asked in earlier years about old China and its modern fate, the Chinese Enlightenment, the survival of Confucianism (see Historic Appendix).[56] Other questions asked about Jews are also linked to the issue of modernity, such as questions about the position of women in Jewish tradition. In China too this is a hot subject. What was the role of women in the modernization of the Jewish people? Do Jews and the Jewish religion know gender discrimination?

The longevity of the Jewish people

The American sinologist Joseph Levenson noted the "paramount importance of historical thinking in Chinese culture."[57] This explains why many Chinese intellectuals are attracted by the longevity and continuity of the Jewish people through three thousand or more years, and like to compare it to their own long history. In a display of traditional Chinese politeness, some affirm to Jewish visitors that the Jews have five thousand years of history and may thus claim even greater age than the Chinese. This can result in a feeling of affinity which few other nations share, and it may even have affected policy when Chinese delegations secretly negotiated with Israel during the 1980s towards the establishment of normal diplomatic relations. The Chinese negotiators mentioned that they and the Jews had the two oldest civilizations, which in their own eyes was one good reason for establishing relations. Of course, the true reason for China's decision was geopolitical and not romantic, but still, the Israeli diplomats involved were amazed that such Chinese fascination with Jews had survived the years of upheaval and revolution, and was now emerging again through diplomats raised under Mao Zedong.[58]

In Christian and Moslem tradition, the longevity of the Jews was never admired, but often denied or presented as Divine punishment. The current political implications of such denials are evident. Late in 2003, the widely read *New York Review of Books* published an attack on Israel — not its policies, but its existence. The author, a well-known, European-born intellectual, called the Jewish state an "anachronism" that should be abolished, because it was allegedly born in nineteenth-century European ideologies. No Chinese who knows his own old history and compares it with that of the Jews, will express such views, whatever his criticism of Israeli policies might be. A Hebrew book, *Jerusalem — 3000 Years of History and Art*, appeared in Chinese in mid-2003, and the first print of 5,000 copies was almost sold out within just a few months. As the denial of Jewish history by enemies of the Jews continues and grows, Jews will appreciate this independent Chinese perspective on their history. It could have weight in the international arena. In general, the Chinese have great interest in their own old history, and many of the popular television soap operas, watched by many millions, have their setting in a remote Chinese past. But books on other old civilizations also sell well. The past can help one make better sense of a confusing present.

Explaining this longevity is not easy. The Chinese wonder how Jews could survive for so long without a land of their own. Their perplexity stems to a large degree from a lack of understanding of the strength of religious beliefs and rituals. An academic author of several books on Jews stated, somewhat incongruously, that the Chinese were not interested in Jewish culture — because they had a great culture themselves — but only in Jewish history. Intellectuals of the prerevolutionary era noted with admiration that the Jews were clinging steadfastly to their "otherness," despite oppression and persecution, which is a valid but not sufficient explanation for longevity. However, the result of this awareness of Jewish longevity is that most Chinese take long-term Jewish survival, both as a people and a state, for granted, and are oblivious of Jewish existential fears and their repercussions on Israeli and Jewish politics.

The *Shoah*

As mentioned in Chapter 4.2, almost as soon as the Chinese discovered the Jews in the late nineteenth century, they also discovered their discrimination and persecution by the West and Czarist Russia. Chinese intellectuals sympathized with Jews because they saw a parallel to their own humiliation. One more hidden reason for Chinese attention to the treatment of the Jews by the "white man" is that it challenged the claim to moral superiority, which an arrogant West added to its already unchallenged military and economic superiority. These reasons have retained their power in the Chinese mind, greatly reinforced by the Nazi *Shoah*. Today, the murder of most European Jews is arguably the most widely known fact of Jewish history. Of the 214 young Beijing students at BFSU who were asked about their views of Jews — none of them students of Jewish or other history — 188 knew of the *Shoah* and some remembered precise facts from movies, books, or school lessons. No other question elicited an equally high proportion of correct answers (Annex 3). Several of China's Judaic scholars first became interested in Jews when they heard of the *Shoah*, some have written books on *Shoah*-related themes, some have organized or planned *Shoah* exhibitions. Many Chinese have seen *Schindler's List*, *The Pianist*, and *Shoah*-related television documentaries. They tend to compare the *Shoah* to their own suffering under Japanese occupation. China's central monument to commemorate its own tragic experience during this period, the *Memorial Hall of the Nanjing Massacre by Japanese Invaders*, emulates in several details the corresponding Jewish monument, the *Yad Vashem* memorial in Jerusalem. It is thus not surprising that some Chinese have noted the current revival of European anti-Semitism, and ask questions of their Jewish visitors from Europe. They are less aware of the links between traditional Western anti-Semitism and anti-Zionism, and do not seem to be informed that the new anti-Semitic wave has a distinctly Islamic color.

7

New Areas of Interest and Old-New Dangers

1. THE RELATIONSHIP WITH CHRISTIANITY AND THE DANGER OF NEW MISCONCEPTIONS

One of the important new, or renewed, areas of Chinese interest pertaining to Jews is the latter's relationship with their two "daughter" religions — Christianity and Islam. To speak of Christianity first, it is true that the Bible was already known in China from the nineteenth century on, and so was its Jewish origin and significance. But the current interest in the Bible is not a straight continuation of past intellectual history; it seems to have new spiritual and sociological roots as well. The views about the importance of the Bible in present-day China diverge widely. Some Chinese experts believe that the Bible is of interest only to a small Christian minority and a few scholars, but to nobody else. Others point to the obvious popularity of illustrated Bible stories, which can indeed be found in all major bookshops. Also, 30 million Bibles (Old and New Testament together) are printed and in circulation in China, which is a larger figure than the officially admitted number of 12 million Chinese Christians. As the standard of living of many Chinese improves and their exposure to foreign influences grows, spiritual interests and questions are likely to become more important. There are credible rumors of a rapid expansion of Christian beliefs and underground churches.

History has shown that the impact of Christianity on the standing of Jews in China can be positive or negative. An indication of negative influences of nineteenth-century missionary activities can be found in hostile comments by the leaders of the Taiping Rebellion, but Christian education also had positive effects for the Jewish people. Two of the most famous Chinese friends of the Jewish people, President Sun Yatsen and the great writer Lin Yutang, heard of the Jews first through their Christian education. Today's Chinese Christians, in China as well as in the United States, are said to have friendly attitudes towards the Jewish people and state.

But it is unclear whether all young readers of the Bible still understand the book as the historic narrative of the Jewish people. For Jewish visitors to China, the most unexpected question asked by students is why the Jews don't accept Jesus. This question was raised several times during the formal question-and-answer sessions with Chinese students (Annex 1). Some think that Jews believe in Jesus, while others simply do not even know that he was a Jew and that

Jews wrote most of the New Testament. A large proportion of graduate students of the School of International Studies of Beijing University did not know that Jesus was a Jew when their professor tested them.[59] Questions about Jesus do not signal dogmatic hostility to Judaism, and interest in Jesus rarely results in formal conversion to Christianity. However, there is little Chinese literature or knowledge on the separation of Christianity from Judaism, on early hostility between Christians and Jews, and on the fundamental differences between the two religions. These are matters that seem to interest some Chinese intellectuals.

The history of Chinese attitudes to Jews could have been dramatically different if the first Christian missionaries to China had not failed, but reached their goal of turning China into a Christian country. The first known texts in the Chinese language that refer to Jews (*Shi-hu*) are Nestorian (Syrian Christian) scrolls of the seventh to eighth centuries, rediscovered in the twentieth century. They narrate Jesus's life and death in a polemical style, paraphrasing some of the more anti-Jewish pages of the Gospels.[60] But the Nestorian church, its Jesus sutras, and missionary activities disappeared in the politically motivated anti-Buddhist sweep of 841–845 and left no mark in Chinese language and thought.

China is opening up to many foreign influences, as it did during the Tang dynasty, which allowed the Nestorians to enter the country. It is likely that Jews will continue to be asked questions about Jesus that are mostly well meaning and not aimed at conversion. The problem is that not all Jews have sufficient knowledge of their own and Christian history to answer these questions. Certainly, Jews must already now pay attention to what Christians teach and write in China. Not all of it is encouraging. For example, the main English Bible text used as teaching material in Beijing's Foreign Studies University describes the history of the Jews in partly respectful, but also partly contemptuous and distorted terms. Many thousands of young Chinese students have read and will keep reading the following phrases, among others:

> We understand how they [the Jewish historians] perverted the truth to increase the glory and the splendor of their own race … Ever since the great exile, the vast majority of the Jewish people had insisted upon living abroad. They were much happier in the cities of Egypt and Greece … where trade was brisk and money flowed freely … The learned scribes who loved to hide the meaning of everything underneath a copious verbiage of Hebrew sentences which created an impression of profound erudition. No … Jesus said: "Thou shalt love the Lord thy God with all thy heart, and with all thy soul …" And, ghastly to contemplate, the whole complicated fabric of Mosaic law would come tumbling down before this terrible new slogan [of Jesus] of "love your neighbor."[61]

2. THE RELATIONSHIP WITH ISLAM AND NEW MOSLEM HOSTILITY

Chinese interest in Islam's relationship with Jews and Judaism is of a different nature and does not seem to have an intellectual prehistory in China, comparable to the earlier interest in the relationship between Judaism and Christianity. Islam had a powerful and uninterrupted presence in China from the eighth century on. Relations between the numerous Moslems and the much fewer Jews of Kaifeng had been notoriously bad at least from the sixteenth century on, as we know from the reports of the Jesuit visitors, but this was generally unknown in, and of no relevance to China.

Today, there is a new Chinese interest in the link between Judaism and Islam that has no roots in past Chinese theological or historic discussions. Chinese scholars, and a part of the public, are more and more interested in the origins of the Arab-Israeli conflict, which fills the news and is a source of great concern, also because of its possible impact on Moslem militancy in China (Chapter 3.2). Increasingly, this interest includes Chinese Arabists and Islam scholars, who often harbor no hostility to Jews or Israel, in contrast to some of their Western colleagues. They understand that the conflict is not simply about borders and settlements, but goes deeper, back to the (often denied) Jewish roots of Islam. Books and university theses on the impact of Judaism on the Koran and Islam are planned or underway. "Studying Islam without knowing Judaism is inadequate," said one of the Islamic scholars of the Institute for World Religions of the Chinese Academy of Social Sciences.[62] Others, in the institutes of international relations that are linked to China's diplomatic community, wonder whether the "common origin" of Judaism and Islam, as some like to see it, will draw the two further apart or closer together. What is important is the willingness of some Chinese scholars to go where some of their Western colleagues still fear to tread. Any genuine scholarly effort in this field deserves strong support. In time, it could give China an independent view of how this conflict began and, perhaps, whether and how it could be settled.

An issue that is different, but very important on its own, is the current attitude of Chinese Moslems to Jews. Some Chinese Moslems harbor an old or new hostility to Zionism or the Jewish people, but this has no link to the very few, barely visible Jews living in China. The hostility has been imported from abroad. Chinese Moslem opposition to the creation of a Jewish state was apparently the main reason why China abstained from voting for the partition of Palestine in the United Nations debate of November 1947.[63] In other words, Chinese Moslem hostility had, and can again have, an influence on Chinese foreign policy. Moslem sensitivities can impinge even on perfectly non-political, scholarly research when it pertains to the Jewish religion. This could be observed in 1993, at a time when the peace process between Israel and the Palestinians seemed to be in full swing. The Shanghai People's Publishing House published an abridged Chinese edition of the *Encyclopaedia Judaica*, to this day the most serious Chinese reference book on Jewish history and culture. In the foreword to the Chinese edition, a vice-president of CASS wrote that Judaism was the "mother religion" of Christianity and Islam. When the first printing was sold out, a second printing was planned, but the ambassador of Saudi Arabia raised an official protest, followed by (more effective) protests by China's own Islamic associations: they claimed that Islam was a new religion that had no links to the Jews. The first official Chinese reaction was to prohibit this second print. The authorities finally relented and allowed the second print, but only on the condition that the editor-in-chief eliminate the CASS foreword that had offended not historic truth, but Wahabi doctrine.

Today, there are Chinese Moslem Web sites that are hostile not only to Israel, but to Jews in general. Chinese Moslems express their opposition to friendly links between China and Israel quite openly, e.g., in television debates. In the BFSU survey of student perceptions of Jews (Annex 3), one of the two Chinese Moslem respondents summarized tersely what he felt about the Jews: "Why don't they die out?" The potential for hostility inside China should not be ruled out.

A Moslem gazette reported on 22 May 2002 that the imam of a mosque in Tianjin was seeking to raise an "army of martyrs" to fight against Israel — until then an unthinkable event in China.[64] Tianjin is not a poor town in a remote Moslem province, but an industrial city of more than 10 million inhabitants that supports one of China's elite universities (Nankai), distanced one hour by train from Beijing. Chinese and Jewish policy makers may have to pay attention to such developments.

3. THE GROWING SHADOW OF THE INTIFADA AND THE CHINESE PUBLIC

The Palestinian Intifada has cast a heavy shadow over the traditional Chinese sympathy for Jews. This is the first Arab-Israeli war that the Chinese have observed since they established diplomatic relations with Israel in 1991. Then, at the time of the Madrid Conference, peace seemed at hand. During earlier wars in the Middle East, Israel was remote. It was a small part of an adversarial Western world, but now it seems much nearer. The official Chinese policy statements are pro-Palestinian. However, it is probably not the statements as such, or China's barely noted pro-Arab votes in the United Nations that had great effects on the Chinese public. What has affected the public mind most is the often one-sided reporting by the state-controlled media, particularly the images of daily violence shown on CCTV (Chinese Central Television) channels.

The Middle East troubles, including those in Iraq, are often the first international news on television and in the Chinese dailies. Every few nights, the Intifada is in hundreds of millions of Chinese living rooms and restaurants. Several Chinese scholars have in the last three years attempted to place articles in newspapers that argue for more balanced understanding for Israel's predicament, but their letters were rejected. In contrast to many European television viewers, Chinese viewers admit that their television is pro-Palestinian. They often give one of two explanations: first, it is alleged that the Chinese always sympathize with the weak, in this case the Palestinians, or second, China is said to partly depend on foreign television reports that are critical of Israel (CNN was mentioned) because the Chinese don't have enough trained journalists in the Middle East. In fact, Chinese scholars do tend to criticize the lack of competence and professionalism of their Middle East journalists, although they know of course that their media are controlled.

Official statements and media reporting have had impacts on public opinion that can be illustrated by the questions asked by some students (Annex 1), and comments written by others (Annex 3). These show disapproval, concern, confusion, and in a minority of cases, a new emotional hostility to Israel, if not to Jews. No non-Israeli Jewish visitor to China can escape the question of Palestine, no matter how often he repeats that he is not an Israeli, and that the aim of his visit is not political. The conflict, or rather the official reaction to it, has brought into focus many questions about who the Jews and the Israelis are, and how the two relate to each other. It has led to questions that were unthinkable before 2000: how could the once-persecuted Jews become "persecutors" or "killers" themselves? The survey of BFSU students (Annex 3) asked: "Do you separate Israeli politics from the Jewish people?" Two contradictory responses (verbatim) are symptomatic of the questions that many other people are asking in China today:

> A: No, I hear that the majority of Israelis are Jewish people.
> B: Yes, they are quite different. Jewish people indeed are quite kind and friendly. But politics are politics, so 'Israeli' is not a pleasant name.

Many Judaic scholars and their students attempt to reassure their Jewish visitors that the Chinese people's sympathy for the Jews remains unaffected, but other evidence does not always support their optimism. The Intifada has not greatly damaged the standing of the Jews in China, but has begun to dent it. It is true that student criticism is voiced by a minority, but it has a stridency that was not heard since the end of the Cultural Revolution a generation ago, then as now triggered by official statements.

Yet the picture is not black and white. Chinese Middle East experts can publish research analyses of the conflict[65] and voice opinions during public television debates that are scholarly and not hostile to Israel. Palestinian suicide bombings have been widely reported and have met with strong official condemnation, also because Chinese citizens living in Israel were among the dead and injured. Even more significant is the recent proliferation of private Chinese Internet online forums. Since 2000–2001, a number of such forums or "chat groups" have been discussing Israel and the Arab-Israeli conflict. Chinese scholars follow these forums closely because they provide a rare insight into what many young Chinese really believe. The chat groups are thought to give an indication of what public opinion among young people and intellectuals might be if there were complete freedom of expression. All scholars who were consulted agreed that the opinions expressed through these Internet forums are overwhelmingly in favor of Israel, and often critical of the Arab world. This does not conform to the position on the Arab-Israeli conflict expressed by the official media.

The official, relatively pro-Arab attitudes to the Intifada could be an issue to be taken up by Jewish organizations. They might be able to argue Israel's case as part of a larger "Jewish People Policy" towards China. Maybe the Chinese authorities would consider concerns about the Chinese media more willingly if non-Israeli Jewish leaders rather than Israelis themselves expressed them. As mentioned above (Chapter 3.2), unbalanced and prominent reporting of the Intifada might have increased anger and militancy in China's Moslem community. In time, it could also have a second negative effect: on the appreciation of the Jewish people by a part of the general Chinese public. Neither effect can be the genuine long-term wish of the Chinese government and people.

4. WESTERN AND JAPANESE ANTI-SEMITISM

Occasional imports of Western and Japanese anti-Semitism into China from the late 1920s to the 1940s have been mentioned in Chapter 4.2 of this report. The emulation of Western trends and values by many young Chinese will make the reappearance of some Western-style anti-Semitism almost inevitable. There is at least one popular, recent Chinese publication on Jewish economic power that has veered off the usual tone of admiration, and adopted more classical anti-Semitic language. Among other things, the book *Unraveling the Secrets of the Exceptional Intelligence of Jews* (1995) teaches the Chinese reader:

> If you do not understand the Jews, you do not understand the world! If Jews sneeze at home, all the banks in the world will one after another get the flu; if three Jews meet together, they can deal in the stock markets of the whole world.[66]

This prose was probably influenced by the recrudescent Japanese anti-Semitism of the 1980s — even the titles of some Japanese books of these years sound suspiciously similar, e.g., Saito Eisaburo's *The Secret of Jewish Power That Moves The World* (1984).[67] But Jewish residents in Hong Kong have reported other and more nasty anti-Semitic manifestations in 2002 and 2003. One such case involved a Chinese bar owner who displayed photos of murdered Jews from a Nazi concentration camp in his bar — to titillate or to shock his customers. At first, the bar owner refused to remove the photographs in spite of Jewish protests. Hong Kong has been under Western influence for far longer than any other important Chinese city, which may explain this particular incident. Certainly, these have been isolated aberrations, which so far have had no influence on the opinion trends of the Chinese majority. Still, it would be erroneous to ignore them completely: combined with other trends, such as possible Moslem animosity, they could become more potent. What is necessary is a Jewish policy effort to convey to the Chinese a realistic image of Jewish economic performance and success, and suggestions as to what others could learn from this success.

8. Chinese Dilemmas and Expectations

1. CHINESE POLICY DILEMMAS

Like many other countries, China has to struggle with conflicting policy objectives. In a historically very short period of twenty-five years, China has emerged as a fast-growing economic powerhouse, it has multiplied its links with the rest of the world, and has begun to respond to the domestic as well as international policy challenges brought about by these changes. Most of the challenges are new for China, and many are daunting. China's leaders have so far tackled them more successfully than many foreign observers had predicted.

The Jewish policy goal of improving the standing of the Jewish people in China and strengthening links with China is intersecting with several Chinese policy objectives. The Jewish goal touches on Chinese policy objectives directly or indirectly, and brings the conflicting nature of some of them to light.

Improving relations with the Jewish people risks bringing into focus China's difficult relations with its own Moslem minority, as well as China's growing interdependence with the Middle Eastern oil producers. On the other hand, closer Chinese-Jewish links could have a beneficial effect on China's relations with the American superpower, the main ally of the Jewish people. In fact, China and the United States are continually searching for common ground, the latter trying to persuade China to become more openly involved both in the war against terrorism and in the Middle East peace process. This would also be in line with many Jewish policy objectives, but it is most unlikely to improve China's relations with the Moslem world inside and outside China, and it might jeopardize old friendships. However, a smooth and mutually beneficial relationship with the United States is an essential precondition for China's fast economic growth, which in turn, is vital if China wants to address its most pressing domestic problems: the increasing wealth gap between the fast-growing coastal regions and the poorer central and Western provinces, and the need to create jobs for more than 100 million "migrant workers." As if these contradictions were not enough, Chinese policies with regard to Jewish religion and descendents are also bedeviled by internal concerns, such as the apprehension of unexpected claims by other small minority groups, and concerns about the influence of foreign sects. Chinese policy hesitations and contradictions resulting from these dilemmas have already become apparent.

2. THE TROUBLE WITH KAIFENG

The trouble with Kaifeng, or better said with the Kaifeng Jewish descendents, can be seen as an example of conflicting policy goals. Since the mid-1990s, the re-emergence of several hundred descendents (their exact number is unknown) demanding recognition of their Jewish ancestry or identity has created delicate policy problems for Chinese and Jews alike. This most isolated of all Jewish communities, discovered by the Jesuit missionary Matteo Ricci in 1605, has fascinated Christians and Jews for a long time, and has also received the attention of Chinese scholars. The community and its synagogue existed at least since the twelfth century, and disintegrated in the nineteenth and early twentieth centuries. Descendents of the original Jewish families in Kaifeng are coming together again, trying to revive some Jewish religious customs, and want to be recognized as a Jewish minority or nationality, *youtai*, and have their status noted on their identity or residence cards. Jewish tourists, particularly from the United States, are encouraging their efforts. The sympathy of Jewish groups from abroad is neither opposed nor encouraged by the Chinese authorities. However, the authorities would prefer to see these revival attempts come to an end, and give no publicity to the few Jewish relics that have remained in the city, but are difficult to find. The official position is that the Jewish descendents have completely assimilated to the Han Chinese, and have disappeared definitively. This position follows a decision taken by the Chinese government in 1953, and repeated since in 1980. In order to give all ethnic groups of China equal rights and a political representation, the government had decided to carry out an effort of ethnic identification and define appropriate criteria for it, as there was no document identifying individual nationalities and the regions they inhabited. The Kaifeng Municipal Government sent two descendents of Jewish families to Beijing to state their case. It turned out, however, that the Jewish descendents did not qualify for recognition according to the criteria adopted for all nationalities. The Central Government document justifying this decision has recently come to light and was translated into English in 2003. It coherently argues the government's case:

> The telegraph dated April 3rd regarding the Kaifeng Jewry is received. Judging from your telegraph, the Jews scattered in Kaifeng have no direct connections economic wise, they don't have a common language of their own, or a common area of inhabitance. They have completely mixed and mingled with the majority Han population, in terms of their political, economical and cultural life, neither do they possess any distinctive traits in any other aspect. All this indicates that it is not an issue to treat them as one distinctive ethnic group, as they are not a Jewish nation by themselves. Secondly, aside from the Kaifeng Jewry, there is a stateless Jewish population in Shanghai. Jewish presence in some other large and middle-sized cities are also possible, however scarce it might be. It is an intricate issue. It could cause other problems and put us in a passive position politically if we acknowledge the Jews of Kaifeng. Therefore, your request of acknowledging Kaifeng Jewry as a separate nationality is improper, based solely on the

historical archival evidence you found. You have only seen the minor, inessential differences between the Kaifeng Jews and their Han counterpart, and failed to see their commonality and the fact that they are essentially the same ... Kaifeng Jewry should be treated as a part of the Han nationality. The major issue is that we should take the initiative to be more caring about them in various activities, and educate the local Han population not to discriminate against, or insult them. This will help gradually ease away the differences they might psychologically and emotionally feel still exists between them and the Han.

The United Front of the Central Committee of the Communist Party of China, June 8th, 1953.[68]

This decision was read and approved by China's four foremost leaders: Chairman Mao, Liu Shaoqi, Zhou Enlai, and Deng Xiaoping, which has made it virtually untouchable, at least for the short and medium term. Considering the period and the context, it must be recognized that this text stands out by a certain sensitivity and fairness. It is unusual in the long history of hostile relations between the Jewish people and the Communist movement, which oscillated between defamation (Marx), anti-Zionism, and anti-Judaism (Lenin), and a planned anti-Semitic genocide (Stalin). The complete absence of anti-Semitic insinuations, and the warnings against insults and discrimination are remarkable in these years when public anti-Semitic insults, discrimination, and persecution reached a peak in the Soviet Union and its satellites (1951–53).[69] As no complaints about insults were known from Kaifeng Jewish descendents, the currently unanswerable question is whether China's Communist leaders wanted to mark their difference from their anti-Semitic "comrades" in Moscow, Warsaw, and Prague. However, the text also leaves no doubt that already in 1953, China grappled with policy conflicts arising from the unique international dimension of the Jewish people. The oblique references to Shanghai, to an "intricate issue", "other problems", and a "passive position" are code words that every Party member would understand. They signaled that China's leaders were uncomfortable with the international implications and links of the Jewish people, and apprehensive about somehow losing control ("passive position") if they gave in on the Kaifeng issue. One should not forget China's international situation at that time: on 8 June 1953, when the document was signed, the war in Korea was still raging. It came to an end on 27 July 1953.

Today, China is concerned not to encourage other small groups to ask for minority status. Henan is a relatively poor and politically difficult province, known for a large and politically strong Moslem community that is not particularly friendly to non-Moslems. Of Kaifeng's approximately 900,000 inhabitants, approximately 150,000 are Moslems. In fact, Kaifeng raises a policy conflict not only for the Chinese but for the Jews as well. Except for a few scholars and intellectuals, Chinese outside Kaifeng have not heard of the Jewish descendents in Kaifeng and their history. Chinese interest in Jews does not focus on Chinese Jews, but on Jews in general. In the BFSU survey of student perceptions of Judaism, Question 3 asked, "What do you know about the history of Jews in China?" (Annex 3).

It is surprising that only eight of the 214 students mentioned Kaifeng, but most of the students knew something about the world history of the Jewish people, particularly the history of persecutions. The difference with Kaifeng, where no such persecutions occurred, should be a source of pride for them, but they were never told. For a Jewish people policy, supporting a group of impoverished Jewish descendents is certainly a noble gesture, but will do nothing to improve the standing of the Jewish people in China, and could even damage it if it triggers new demands from other small minorities and raises serious problems for the authorities. The sympathy and help that the group certainly deserves must not come at the expense of broader Jewish policy objectives. Foreign intervention will currently not modify Chinese national, Henan provincial, or Kaifeng municipal policies in this question, but time might bring about change.

A different matter is the awareness and study of old Jewish history in China from the twelfth to the nineteenth century. This is an extremely interesting chapter of Jewish as well as Chinese history that Jews have neglected for too long (see Historic Appendix). Important questions relating to this chapter of history await further research. Jewish policy should encourage the study of the old history of Chinese Jews and promote greater Chinese awareness of it, not only for academic reasons, but because this history testifies to the very old bonds between the Chinese and Jewish peoples. Also, the more recent history of the Jewish descendents, for example during the Cultural Revolution, and their present socio-economic conditions might merit sociological research. An international symposium held in 2003 at the University of Mainz in Germany has made interesting academic contributions to this issue, among others.[70]

3. OTHER ECHOES OF POLICY CONFLICTS

There are other examples of policy conflicts. Israel's cultural policy, particularly the funding of Chinese books on Jewish culture and history, has greatly "unnerved" the Arab embassies, to quote the director of one of the main Chinese institutes of international relations. In contrast to some skeptical Jewish observers, the Arab countries have no doubt about the potentially deep impact of cultural policies in China, and have expressed unhappiness about the numbers of Israeli delegations and visitors. Chinese scholars, who need to maintain good relations with all sides, have hinted that it is sometimes easier for them to meet with international Jewish, rather than Israeli visitors.

Chinese censorship shows the effects of these dilemmas. The National Bureau of Publications checks books and articles on sensitive subjects, such as religion, minority affairs, diplomatic issues, and recent Chinese history. Since the beginning of the Intifada, books on Jewish subjects, including religion, culture, old history, Bible, etc., have to be submitted, as well as books on Islam and the Arab world, and censorship has become more restrictive. Books can be banned entirely, or parts of them can be deleted. In general, translations of foreign authors pass much more easily than new books by Chinese authors. The latter, of course, resent these practices, which seem to them often erratic and unclear.

Another problem is a lack of information coordination and cooperation between the

Judaic scholars of China. The time would be ripe for them to set up a national association of Judaic scholars of China, with a regular bulletin, an annual meeting, etc. The scholars are aware of the need. The obstacles are partly financial, as the organization of bulletins and meetings has to be funded, but there are also political problems that have nothing to do with Jewish studies as such. The Chinese authorities are reluctant to approve the setting up of new cross-national associations of any kind because they are apprehensive about emulation by unwanted sects. Again, Jewish policy interests intersect and risk conflicting with other Chinese policy priorities.

A more severe problem that hampers the effectiveness of a Jewish cultural and information policy is linked to the lack of transparency of the Chinese book market. This is a systemic problem affecting all publications and many fields of scholarship in China. It is mentioned here, although it is impossible to say whether it is worse or better for Jewish books compared to others, and whether this is another example of a policy conflict, or simply the result of China's different cultural traditions. Many books on Jewish themes have been selling well, but it is impossible to know who bought them, which are still available, and where they could be bought, and almost impossible to learn which books have just appeared or will soon appear — except by browsing in the large bookshops of the main cities. China has no commercial organization comparable to Amazon.com, and even the largest bookshops in Shanghai have information only on books they keep currently in stock themselves. It is a common complaint of Chinese intellectuals, even scholars, that they cannot find books on Jews or the Middle East, or not the books they need. It is an equally common complaint by authors of Jewish subjects that publishing is very difficult in China in general, and that their publishers do not want to reprint sold-out books even if there is still demand for them. Is this due to lack of transparency, financing or other imperfections of the market system, or due to restrictive interventions by government authorities that are specifically aimed at books on Jewish and Middle Eastern subjects? In the latter case, this would again point to a policy dilemma. The classical method of publicizing new books is by reviews in newspapers and magazines. But in China, such reviews are scarce. However, there are regular book fairs in the large cities, particularly Shanghai, where books on Jewish themes have been displayed.

4. CHINESE EXPECTATIONS

The Chinese will attempt to reduce the potential for policy conflicts that could arise from their relations with the Jewish people, and will, quite naturally, use these relations for their own interests and policy goals. Jewish policy goals, as described at the beginning of this report, must be aware of what the Chinese expect from the Jews, whether these expectations are officially stated or not. Because the Chinese believe that the Jews have power and influence, they also believe that they have a lot to give. This expectation appeared in the comments both of university experts and students. It is quite surprising that almost fifty of the 214 interviewed BFSU students stated that Jews are "important" or "very important" in China, although no indigenous, and only relatively few foreign Jews are living in the country (Annex 3). It is essential for a successful Jewish policy to identify where Jews can and should respond to Chinese expectations.

a. China wants to have the support of the American Jewish community in managing and improving China's crucial, but complex and oscillating relationship with the United States. Virtually every Chinese interested in politics — government members, professors, students — is convinced that American Jews are very powerful, in politics, the economy, science, culture, and defense. In Chinese eyes, "Jewish power" has nearly mythical dimensions. Widely traveled professors of international relations express the hope that "the Jews" will help manage the difficult relations between China and the United States. A graduate student in Shanghai asked in November 2003 what role the "famous Jewish lobby groups" were playing in the trade disputes between the two countries — were they for or against China? (Annex 1). The idea that "the Jews" might have no position at all on a subject of great concern to him did not even cross his mind. Many Chinese would like to understand how "the Jewish lobby" became the apparently most influential pressure group in American politics, followed, allegedly, by the "Taiwan lobby."[71] A stable, more friendly and beneficial relationship with the United States would go a long way to make up for frictions that China might have to incur in its relations with the Moslem world. An example of how American Jews could help is provided in Chapter 3.3 — by cooperation with Chinese Americans who fight against hostile stereotypes that are very similar to those from which Jews often suffered. Chinese representatives in the United States are seeking links with Jewish organizations; they are wooing the Jews of America, which could give the latter some strategic leverage. Israel, in contrast, is wooing China — not quite the same situation.

b. China wants continued access to Israel's advanced technologies, particularly in fields related to agriculture, telecommunications, and defense. Many Chinese respect the Jews because they know of the contributions that Israeli agricultural, drip irrigation, and solar energy technologies have made to China's development. They see in these contributions an expression of "Jewish culture" or "cultural inventiveness."[72] Some Chinese also emphasize that Israel has helped the Chinese military.

c. As mentioned above, the Arab-Israeli conflict is becoming a growing source of concern because of China's increasing dependence on Middle Eastern oil and concern about Moslem militancy in China itself. When President Hu Jintao told visiting Israeli President Moshe Katsav during a meeting at the Great Hall of the People on 18 December 2003 that the "Israeli-Palestinian issue had been left unsettled for over half a century, and brought disaster to all nations and their peoples…,"[73] he expressed a degree of Chinese unhappiness that is widely shared. The Chinese hope that Israeli policies will not negatively affect China's sensitive interests, and sometimes assume that Jewish visitors are an appropriate, additional channel through which to convey their concerns and hopes to Israel.

d. The Chinese stereotype that Jews are the economically most successful and affluent of all peoples, naturally leads some persons to hope for direct Jewish contributions to China's development. Jewish businessmen or Jews in senior positions in international corporations are investing in China. However, with a few exceptions, such investments do not appear as "Jewish" because they are classified by national, not religious-cultural origin. There is no shortage of investment money in China. What the Chinese seek from the Jews, apart from Israeli technology, is perhaps more their international connections and a better understanding of the world economy. A Chinese scholar, who is studying the economic power of American Jews, was disappointed that he could not find comprehensive, professional literature on this subject.[74]

e. There are never enough funds for all the teaching, research, and publication activities on Judaism that would be possible in Chinese academic institutions. In line with Chinese views about Jewish financial power, the Chinese expect the Jewish people to fund a large part of these activities. It should be added that many foreign countries are helping to finance intellectual and cultural endeavors in China. For example, it is no great secret that the Arab world is helping to finance the study of Arab language and Middle Eastern issues in academic institutions.

f. Somewhat surprisingly, there are appeals to Jewish generosity that are not linked to the funding of Judaic scholarship in China or to Jewish economic investments. These appeals result from a feeling that the Chinese people could expect more recognition from the Jewish people for having allowed Jewish refugees to find a new home in Shanghai and Harbin when few were doing so in the West. One Chinese policy advisor did not like some documentary films about the Jews of Shanghai because they never mentioned the Chinese people. In fact, Jews must understand that the notion of "gratitude" is essential in Chinese tradition and behavior. The concept can work both ways; one official pointed out that China was grateful to Israel "to this very day" for having recognized the People's Republic of China in January 1950, long before most other countries. The Chinese public and intellectuals are probably not aware that individual Jews have made charitable donations in China.

g. Last but not least, some Chinese would like to learn from the Jews more than just how to become rich. When some authorities or colleagues questioned the work of Judaic scholars, calling their interest exaggerated and not justified by China's real problems, they replied that China has much to learn from the history of Jewish survival and success, and that studying Jewish history is in China's own national interest. One scholar quoted from the statement of the 2003 Plenary Session of the Chinese Communist Party that called for greater efforts to "foster the Chinese spirit and civilization." The scholar added that the Chinese must study the Jewish experience for the reconstruction of their own culture, because the Jews have shown the way towards successful assimilation of foreign cultures. Chinese students have often asked what the Chinese could "learn" from the Jews, and their minds were certainly not set on money (Annexes 1 and 3).

9 Jewish Policy Challenges

1. POSSIBLE POLICY DISSONANCES WITH CHINA

The Chinese expectations that have been enumerated are policy challenges for the Jewish people. Positive Jewish responses would serve Jewish as well as Chinese goals. There is common ground, which is why many of the policy recommendations at the beginning of this report are also responses to Chinese expectations. A general problem that the Chinese and Jews will encounter is that they often tend to think in different time frames. The Chinese time frame is long, the Jewish short, which can lead to dissonances of expectations. Mindful of their own policy dilemmas, China's policy makers might be slow in reacting to Jewish policy initiatives and hesitant in making major decisions. They will follow time-honored Chinese tradition and pursue a "wait-and-see" attitude, avoiding sudden changes. In contrast, the Jewish public and policy makers generally wish to see quick results and success. China's first ambassador to Israel, who got to know the Jews and their problems very well, has good advice:

> The future will be long; our two civilizations have thousands of years of history. Go step by step, don't be in a hurry, have confidence in yourselves ...[75]

However, a policy limited to pragmatic step-by-step approaches will strengthen some areas of mutual understanding and interest, but will not necessarily remove areas of chronic, or future policy dissonances between Chinese and Jews. These areas must not be ignored. Only a strategic, long-term Jewish people policy can anticipate and address them in time.

- The Chinese belief in Jewish power in the United States could become a double-edged sword and a source of severe disappointment if there is ever a sharp deterioration of American-Chinese relations. This is particularly true if this deterioration reveals the limits of Jewish power — or of Jewish willingness to help China. The possibility of a real crisis, even a military conflict in the long term, seems remote, but it is still openly discussed in China, including in television talk shows — as it is in the United States (Chapter 3.3). It is interesting — if not worrying — that some scholars specializing in Jewish studies mention a conflict with the United States as inevitable, one quoting an ancient Chinese proverb: "There cannot be more than one tiger on the same mountain."

- The issue of Taiwan, even short of a military conflict between China and the United States, could become an area of dissonance in case of major American or Chinese policy shifts. An alleged threat to Taiwan by China was the reason why the United States forced Israel to break the "Falcon" contract with China (Chapter 3.3). Independent of their essential alliance with America, Jews have no historic interest or stake in Taiwan. When Israel's government, ahead of most other countries, recognized the People's Republic of China in 1950, it made a fundamental decision regarding the unity of China, which has never been challenged by Jewish leaders. However, as Taiwan is lobbying hard for American Jewish support, Jewish leaders must never forget that their support for Israel and wish to strengthen the links between the Jewish people and China on the one hand, and hypothetical political support for Taiwan on the other, would be conflicting objectives.

- Human rights issues are one of the obstacles to improving relations between China and the United States, and this inevitably involves Jewish policy positions. The fight of Jewish organizations against anti-Jewish discrimination anywhere in the world has always been supported by the United States, and it is generally linked with human rights concepts that Jews cannot and will not abandon. But Jews could make an original contribution to a human rights discussion with China. Many modern human rights are rooted in Jewish biblical traditions, e.g., the sanctity of human life concept. Talmudic and rabbinic law developed human rights concepts and applications that are essential to normative Judaism, but not identical to the modern international human rights conventions. The Chinese have made similar claims for themselves. It can indeed be shown that China has a rich and distinct rights discourse going back many centuries.[76] Based on their own spiritual history, Jews can accept that there may be more than just one single proper concept of human rights, and that communication between those holding different concepts and believing in their wider value, is not only possible, but necessary.

- Apart from the issue of Kaifeng (Chapter 8.2), some Jews would like China to recognize the Jewish religion in some official way. Other Jews strongly disagree that this should be a Jewish policy goal. There are Orthodox observant Jews in China, but they are foreigners who are treated like all other foreigners. Orthodox Jewish practice is unhindered and free in China, including ritual slaughter under rabbinical supervision, circumcision, private Jewish education, etc. There might be policy dissonances with regard to the issue of recognition within the Jewish community, more than between China and the overwhelming majority of Jews.

- China's votes in the United Nations and its various bodies have consistently supported the Arab and Moslem states against Israel, whatever the contexts. While Israel's isolation in the United Nations is a source of unhappiness for Jews, China's position has barely been noted because it is identical to that of many others. Beijing has used its pro-

Arab votes as a counterweight, if not a cover, for its good relations with Israel. As long as there is no radical tilt of Chinese policy towards the Arab and Moslem world, e.g., one involving future transfers of blueprints or components for unconventional weapons, the dissonance at the United Nations is likely to remain bearable.

2. CHINESE OPPORTUNITIES AND NEEDS

The wish of many Chinese to learn more from and about the Jews is a key component of the above-mentioned Chinese expectations (Chapter 8). It is the knowledge that the Jews have (e.g., Israeli technology, Jewish economic skills), and the knowledge of how the Jews acquired their know-how and success (Jewish power in America, Jewish modernization) that are so attractive. Chinese interest is an opportunity for the Jews, but Jewish responses have been insufficient. In 1997–1998, a Judaic scholar from the Chinese Academy of Social Sciences (CASS) described the prevailing information situation as very unsatisfactory:

> ...There is still a great shortage of high-quality academic books, translations and articles on Jewish history, culture, scripture, ethics, law, mysticism, philosophy, contemporary thought etc. In order for the subject of Jewish studies to develop greater breadth and depths, there is still a need for more investment of research, a greater number of specialized organizations and personnel etc.[77]

In spite of progress in several fields, the situation today is not substantially different. Many of the surveyed BFSU students (107 of 214) affirm that they are eager to learn more about Jews and Jewish culture (Annex 3), but some are painfully aware of their main constraint: "I don't have the resources."[78]

The discussion in this paper has shown that research organizations, scholars, and students seek more information on Jewish topics. More than one academic institution would like to create a Jewish culture or history center, or one on Middle East studies, and several want to expand already existing activities in these areas. Most are looking for Jewish or other links and support, but many have difficulties in identifying or contacting the right persons abroad. Scholars plan new books about Jewish themes. Others have plans for exhibitions (e.g., on the *Shoah*), seminars, workshops, Jewish culture weeks, and Jewish film and theater presentations. Many more students would like to learn Hebrew than is currently possible: in 2003, one hundred students applied to the Modern Hebrew Language class of BEIDA (University of Beijing), but only twelve were admitted. Other universities, e.g., in Shanghai and Jinan, would like to set up or expand Hebrew language classes but are short of competent teachers and resources. Many scholars and students of Jewish topics would like to meet Jews or visit Israel. Some have said that they encountered difficulties.

What do Chinese decision makers and opinion leaders know about Jews and the origins of the Middle East conflict, and do they see a need to learn more? An effort was made to clarify this issue by indirect means, but no comprehensive picture emerged from the interviews conducted for this report, except that the importance of scholars as policy advisors is probably increasing (Chapter 5.2). Does an interest in Judaic studies point to needs that are felt at senior policy levels? Some of the interviewed experts and opinion makers with contacts at such levels were well informed about the Jewish people, but others were not, and some were woefully misinformed, occasionally even about Jews in China. Some Chinese experts do need more accurate information, but whether they are aware of it is another matter. An important recommendation for Jewish policy makers would be to encourage and fund more study tours of Chinese scholars, students, and officials to Israel, the United States or other countries, with the aim of familiarizing them with Jewish topics.

In general, there is little need to stimulate more interest in Jewish matters in China. The interest is there. The question is how to respond to it.

3. JEWISH POLICY SHORTCOMINGS

Jewish policies have responded to some opportunities and needs in China, but not to others. This shortcoming results, first of all, from the fact that the "Jewish people" is not a state or a coherent entity. It has neither a government nor a parliament. It is a complex, multinational, self-organizing entity with many cooperating but also competing branches and bodies. Can such a protean people have "policies"? Can it define and carry out a coherent policy supported by many Jews? Or could it only have different, conflicting policies? The last hundred years have demonstrated that both single and multiple policies are possible. Today, both the State of Israel and Jewish people bodies have policies. These are rarely identical. More often, they are somewhat coordinated, but distinct. There is not enough information coordination and cooperation between Jewish groups worldwide, between the United States and Israel, and also between groups inside the United States. The multiplicity of Jewish interests and initiatives testifies to the vitality of Jewish life. Inevitable as this multiplicity is, it can put Jews at a disadvantage when dealing with a better-coordinated and hierarchical country that has long-term political objectives.

How often in history was the Jewish people prepared to take a long-term view, anticipate events, and prepare for the future? An astute Chinese observer of Jewish history, the Bible scholar Qiu Zihua, examined in 1990 the general characteristics of the "Hebrew national spirit." Although he did not use the word "policy", his conclusion amounted to saying that Jews were never good at policy-making:

> The Hebrew nation exercised patience, and was of a tough and persevering character, but it was often passive in attending to business, and often neglected taking the initiative in dealing with challenges in its surroundings.[79]

With regard to China, there was Israel's forward-looking recognition of the People's Republic in 1950, and Ben-Gurion's efforts to establish links with the great civilizations of Asia. But apart from these early visionary moments, the policies of Jewish people bodies have been mostly short-term and pragmatic, which was inevitable in a context of almost continuous emergencies and threats. These policies were concerned with Jews where they lived, and with the problems and dangers they faced, rather than with the long-term strategic importance of remote powers. This seems to be changing now, albeit slowly. Coherent long-term policies to respond to threats as well as opportunities are still not well developed. It must also be said that many Jewish leaders and most Jews are still completely unaware that there is considerable Chinese interest in Jewish issues.

Lack of information is a part and a result of policy shortcomings, and so is shortage of funds. It would be tempting to begin with the practical needs, trying to spread more information on Chinese Judaic research and teaching, and collect more money. In the long term, this is not the right approach. A comprehensive, new effort has to begin with policy, not information or money, because a coherent strategy will by itself increase the flow of information and facilitate the raising of new funds. Jewish academics who did raise money for Sino-Judaic links have been explicit about this: more money could be found if a competent body would produce a relevant and compelling policy report on the issue.[80] Still, money is obviously a critical problem. With more money, many expectations could be met, and more good projects carried out. Apart from the Chinese academic sector providing the infrastructure, the funding sources for Judaic scholarship and information were mainly Jewish. Funding came from Israel (government, industry, and the private organization *Igud Yotzei Sin*, former Jewish residents of China), and from American or other private foundations. An important non-Jewish source was Germany, which funded several international symposia on Jews and China. One of the long-term tasks of a Jewish policy will be to increase the number of funding sources. These should eventually include more international non-Jewish funding agencies, as well as Chinese industry.

A part of the current problem is a cutback in Israel's cultural policy in China, which could be observed from 2001 on. In principle, this report is not charged with reviewing Israeli policy. However, Israel's cultural activities were once the Jewish people's best-known and most audible voice in China, and therefore cannot be omitted from a Jewish people policy frame. Israel used culture as a medium to create stronger links between China and the Jewish people, but cultural policy has been affected by changing priorities and budget cuts imposed by a difficult economic and security situation. Money is not the only issue. Israel's support for book translations, annual scholarships, and other endeavors continues to be greatly appreciated, but some Judaic centers in more remote Chinese provinces are looking for Jewish advice, links, or visits, which have not been forthcoming in 2003. Does Israel currently have a coherent long-term cultural policy with regard to China, and does this policy have a Jewish content and purpose? Or are policy and prioritizing left to the initiative of individual, changing diplomats? Considering Chinese views of Jewish history and culture, is it a "Jewish" priority to show in China contemporary Israeli art?

These and other questions could be part of a critical policy assessment and long-term policy strategy as advocated several times by this report. They should lead to policy recommendations that are pragmatic and actionable, even if some of them, as proposed at the beginning of the report, might also be very demanding.

ANNEX 1. Questions asked by Students following S. Wald's Conferences in Chinese Universities, October and November 2003

The questions quoted below were raised by Chinese students during question-and-answer sessions, following the conferences on Jewish culture that the author of this report held in six universities. The student interest was overwhelming. Students wanted to raise many more questions than the allocated time allowed. Very few of these young Chinese had ever met a Jew, and none had the same easy access to information and literature as Western students have. Yet many of their questions were searching and sophisticated. Many were also sympathetic, while others, related to the Middle East conflict that preoccupies young Chinese, were critical, and a few were openly hostile. While many of the attending students were studying Jewish subjects, many others came from other fields. Together, their questions give a small, fascinating snapshot of the thoughts of some young Chinese who will become part of the future elite of China.

A. *Beijing University (BEIDA), School of Foreign Languages, Hebrew Language class, 24 October 2003. Teacher: Dr. Wang Yu et al., fifteen students and teachers.*
   Conference theme: "Program and Goals of the Jewish People Policy Planning Institute."

1. How can we find a way to study in Israel?
2. Why can't we make friends with Israelis?
3. How can we get Jewish pen friends?

B. *University of Henan, Kaifeng, Institute of Jewish Studies, 31 October 2003. Teacher: Prof. Zhang Qianhong et al., thirty students and teachers.*
   Conference theme: "Program and Goals of the Jewish People Policy Planning Institute."

1. What is the situation of the Kibbutz today? How does the Kibbutz compare with similar Chinese experiences?
2. Bible Scholar: We have been working on Judaism and Biblical literature for so long and are still isolated. What can we do to be better known?
3. What are the similarities between Jewish and Chinese culture?
4. Why have the Jewish and Chinese civilizations survived, but not those of ancient Egypt and India?
5. What are the major differences between Judaism and Confucianism?
6. How about Palestine? Will there be a Palestinian state in the future?

7. Jews are richer and cleverer than many others. What is the reason for their success? Can you give me practical advice on how I can learn more about the Jews?

C. *Yunnan University, Kunming, School of International Relations, 4 November 2003. Teacher: Prof. Xiao Xian et al., thirty students and teachers.*

Conference theme: "Israel and Diaspora Judaism — History and Current Trends."

1. What is the attitude of French Jews to Israel's policy under Sharon?
2. What is your personal attitude to Israel's unlawful settlement activities?
3. Where do you feel more as a foreigner, in Israel or in Europe?
4. Sharon said in a speech to European visitors that he wants to bring one million more Jews to Israel. Does this mean more settlements in the territories?
5. Why does Israel help India with military equipment? Why this alliance between Israel and India?
6. Do you have a double loyalty? Do you feel more French and European, or more Israeli?
7. What are the relations between France and Israel today?
8. In the past, Israel had good relations with Africa. Does Israel still play a positive role in Africa's development?
9. You said in your speech that Jews are potentially stronger today than they have been in the past. In what sense are they stronger?

D. *Shandong University, Jinan, Institute for Jewish Studies, 7 November 2003. Teacher: Prof. Fu You-de et al., fifteen students and teachers.*

Conference theme: "Program and Goals of the Jewish People Policy Planning Institute."

1. What has been the effect of the Holocaust on Jewish faith today?
2. Can you define the essence of Jewish ethics?
3. What is the essence of Jewish ritual? Ritual as such cannot be so important — what is behind this ritual?
4. What is the link between the core beliefs of Judaism and the external ritual?
5. Why did the Chinese in past history treat Jews better than the Europeans, allowing them to make official careers in China?
6. What is the image of Jews in today's Europe? How do Jews identify themselves and think of themselves, in today's Europe?
7. If you don't believe in God but do good deeds, can you still be considered as a Jew?
8. Are there any spiritual links between the Karaites and the Sadducees, as both rejected the Oral Law?

E. *Shanghai Academy of Social Sciences, Center of Jewish Studies, 11 November 2003. Teacher: Prof. Pan Guang et al., thirty-forty students and teachers.*

Conference theme: "History and Political Power of American Judaism."

1. What can be done against the growth of anti-Semitism in Europe and America since 11 September 2001?

2. Malaysia's Mahathir Mohammed said that the Jews control the world. When a Jew seeks power, does he do this because he is a Jew, or simply because he likes power?
3. What is the influence of American Jews on U.S. policies in the Middle East, and on the "Road Map" in particular?
4. The influence of Jewish lobby groups in the U.S. is well known. Sino-American trade relations are accompanied by increasing American pressures on China. What role — for or against China — do Jewish lobby groups play in Sino-American trade disputes?
5. Jews are famous for their generous contributions to Jewish causes. Shanghai has done a lot for Jews when the city gave them a safe haven during World War II, but Jews have never made any donation to Shanghai. Why not?

F. *Nanjing University, all Faculties, 13 November 2003. Teacher: Prof. Xu Xin et al., more than four hundred students and teachers.*

Conference theme: "Cross-cultural Comparisons between the Chinese and the Jewish Civilization."

1. You mentioned the history of Jewish suffering. What did the Jews learn from their own suffering? Do they have understanding for the suffering of the Palestinians? [Booing and catcalls by many other students.]
2. Jesus said to you: If you believe in me as your savior, you do no longer need a land — you carry the land in your heart. Why then do the Jews keep fighting with the Arabs about the land over there? [Again, booing and catcalls by many other students.]
3. What can the Chinese learn from Jewish history, and vice versa?
4. What impact will the Jewish Enlightenment (*Haskalah*) have on Jewish history in the next one hundred years?
5. You mentioned "Chinese suffering" at the hand of the Mongols and Manchus when the Song and Ming dynasties were overthrown. But who is "Chinese" for you? Only Han people? Is nobody else "Chinese"? [In fact, China today considers the Mongols and Manchus as Chinese nationalities that are equivalent to the Han majority.]
6. What is the most important thing in life for you — the economy or religion? [This woman student had read the speaker's CV and noted that he had degrees in economics and history of religion.]
7. Can you explain the large number of brilliant Jews in all fields of knowledge?
8. Why did you always speak of a "Jewish civilization" and never mentioned religion? The main characteristic of Judaism is that it is a religion believing in one God. The Chinese have various religions with different gods. What is the effect of this difference on Chinese and Jews?
9. If Jews in general have survived for so long, why did the Jews of Kaifeng disappear?

G. *Nanjing University, Graduate students (history, literature, religion), 14 November 2003. Teacher: Prof. Xu Xin et al., approximately sixty students and teachers.*

Conference theme: "Judaism: Civilization or Religion?"

1. Many great persons were Jews — we respect Jews very much. But the Chinese love peace. What then is the chance that the war in Israel could be ended soon? The Chinese perception of Jews would improve.
2. Has the wisdom or intelligence of the Jews anything to do with their Judaism?
3. You are the first Jew I see. Jews are an "awesome" people [said in English]; committed, proud, persistent. But your existence is a paradox. For your wisdom and persistence, your country should be the main instrument to secure your civilization — but Israel is still in danger. As I am the first woman to speak here, my question is: What have women contributed to Jewish civilization, and particularly to its modernization?
4. We don't know the Jewish perspective on China, and when we think of Jews, we mean mainly American Jews. Should a conflict break out between China and the U.S., where will the Jews stand?
5. The most impressive Jew in history was Jesus. When Buddha appeared in India, the Brahmans rejected him, like the Jews rejected Jesus. But later on, Hinduism finally accepted Buddha as an incarnation of the god Brahma. Why can't Jews accept Jesus, e.g., as an incarnation of Abraham?
6. What does the concept of a "Chosen People" mean? Is there any modernization of this concept?
7. Is there any Chinese influence on the Jews of America and Israel, and what could such influence achieve?
8. Can China learn any lessons from the long history of conflict between tradition and modernity in Judaism?
9. What is the impact of Judaism on Jewish economic activities and success?
10. How do you view the history of Nazism?
11. What is the influence of religion and culture on the Middle East conflict?
12. Why did the "canonization" of the *Torah* take place while the Persians ruled the Middle East? Is there a link?
13. Is anti-Semitism a culture conflict?
14. What was the role of the Big Powers in the creation of Israel?
15. What is considered the most important value in Judaism?

ANNEX 2. Titles of Essays on Jewish History and Culture submitted by Students of the University of Henan in Kaifeng in Summer 2003

These papers are the result of an essay competition organized in Summer 2003 by Professor Zhang Qianhong, Director of the Institute of Jewish Studies of Henan University in Kaifeng, created in 2002. The honorary director of the institute, Mr. Len Hew, a Canadian Chinese, provided funding. All students, not only those of the Jewish Studies institute, were invited to participate by contributing a paper of at least three thousand Chinese characters on a freely chosen subject of Jewish culture or history. The students were invited to use the institute's Judaica library (comprising close to one thousand volumes) for this purpose. Prizes were offered for papers of quality. Forty papers were submitted at short notice. None of them was hostile, ten were eliminated, and thirty received a prize. The first, second, and third prizes consisted of money; the honor prize was a book on Judaism. The text of ten selected essays, and the names of all thirty prizewinners, as well as the titles of their papers, were published in the university journal. Following the success of this initiative, in January 2004, the Institute of Jewish Studies published a notice for a second competition, in order to encourage more young Chinese to undertake Judaic studies. This competition took place in April 2004, with almost three times as many participants as in 2003; ninety-eight essays were submitted.

A review of the titles of the 2003 competition (below) reveals an impressive degree of originality, sympathy, and sophistication, and a broad range of interests by these young Chinese. This is more than what one might expect in one of the less developed inland provinces of China, only one year after the establishment of the first Institute of Jewish Studies. It should be noted that the existence of the historically once-famous Jewish community in Kaifeng had no influence on the interests of these students, with one exception only. None of the descendents of this community is among the students.

FIRST PRIZE:

Not attributed.

SECOND PRIZES:

1. Zhao Guanggui, "About Voters and Anti-Semitism"
2. Yan Meng, "Bliss or Tragedy? On Jewish History"
3. Ren Yanrong, "On the Impact of Greek Civilization on Jewish Civilization"

4. Li Yong/Wang Dakai, "The Status of Post-War Russian Judaism in the Zionist Movement"

THIRD PRIZES:

5. Xu Zhenjiang, "Growing Civilization in the Diaspora"
6. Huo Xiaoling, "An Inexhaustible Source: What Can We Learn from It?"
7. Peng Xiaoming, "Jewish Culture: Radiating on Top of World Literature"
8. Hua Man, "From a Cradle of Culture to a Cultural Desert"
9. Chu Xiuhong, "Looking at the Jews with a View on Shylock's Destiny"
10. Li Ziqing, "The Final Separation of Christianity from Judaism"
11. Liu Tongli, "About the Israeli Kibbutz — A Modern Utopia"

HONOR PRIZES:

12. Qin Rongqing, "On Jewish Medical Science"
13. Guo Yingying, "Comparisons between Traditional Chinese and Jewish Education"
14. Wang Dongmei, "Several Reasons why America Supported Israel"
15. Zhang Nana, "The Jews and Money — A Weird Cycle"
16. Meng Jie, "My Understanding of the Assimilation of the Jews of Kaifeng"
17. Wang Huanxin, "Brutal Nazis — Devastated Jews. Why?"
18. He Shujie, "Jewish Family Education"
19. Feng Lixia, "About Israeli Education"
20. Liu Junxia, "Shanghai's Schindler in the Second World War"
21. Li Gang, "The Sources of Anti-Semitism"
22. Wang Shunxiao, "Thoughts on the Ups and Downs of the Jewish National Movement"
23. Pan Xiyan, "On Intermarriage of the Jews"
24. Hou Liangliang, "American Attitudes towards Israeli-Chinese Diplomatic Ties when China was Newly Founded"
25. Zhang Chunyan, "About the Origin of Black Jews"
26. Zhang Fu, "How Jewish Culture was Formed"
27. Yang Fan, "The Kibbutz — A Model of Jewish Communism"
28. Chen Zhiquan, "Dispersed but Enduring: The Jews"
29. Ma Yuan, "Brave and Courageous Jews"
30. Xie Chunsheng, "The Definition of a Jew"

ANNEX 3. Beijing College Students' Understanding of Judaism

The following summary was written by Lauren Katz, an American who studied in 2003 in Beijing. It is based on a survey of Chinese students that she designed and carried out from October to December 2003. Most of the interviewed students were from the Beijing Foreign Studies University, BFSU. This is China's best foreign language university, which has students from all over China. This and other top-level universities are currently training China's future professional and political elites. None of the students studied Judaism, any other religion or history, and none had probably ever met a Jew. This is the first known survey on Chinese perceptions of Jews. It is not a "sample" in a quantitative statistical sense, but a qualitative review that provides supporting evidence for information received from other sources. It gives a fascinating insight into what a number of students in Beijing think and say about Jews, but should not be used as proof of any particular thesis.

Eight questions were asked. Quotes below are left as they were written, without correcting the students' English mistakes.

Number of participating students: 214.

Sex: 60 male, 147 female, 7 no response.

Age: 17 (4), 18 (29), 19 (23), 20 (35), 21 (6), 22 (27), 23 (5), 24 (3), 25 (1), 26 (1), 27 (1), 34 (1), 35 (1) [the 34- and 35-year-olds are professors].

Religion: No Response: 63[81], None: 128, Marxist: 2, Confucianist: 2, Buddhist: 5, Moslem: 2, Christian: 3, Dualist: 1, Zhejiang: 1, Han: 1[82]

1. RESEARCH METHOD

The survey was conducted to find out how Chinese college students perceive Jewish people and what they know about Judaism. Questionnaires were distributed at informal gatherings in places such as the English Corner at Beijing Foreign Studies University (BFSU)[83] and to random students on campus. As the questionnaire was written in English, the students had to have some proficiency in English to participate. Out of 214 replies, thirteen were returned in Chinese and had to be translated into English. The survey results may have a "liberal" bias because BFSU is a foreign language university with a larger international student population than most Chinese universities, which is likely to encourage Chinese students towards greater openness. This also means that these students will probably play leading professional roles in

China in the next generation. Further related research included consulting BFSU students' textbooks and reference books to better understand the students' access to information.

2. MAIN THESIS

The understanding of Judaism and the Jewish people by these Chinese college students is significant, considering that it is often derived from stereotypes and that the limited written and audiovisual resources available are generally controlled by the Chinese authorities.

3. ANALYSIS OF SURVEY RESULTS

Question 1:
What is your knowledge of Jewish culture and religion?

A typical answer:

"I'm sorry, I know little about Jews. I've just heard that Jews are clever and are good at business. They were forced to leave their homes and traveled to lead a life. Germans hated Jews (I suppose) and killed a lot of them."

Example of a sophisticated answer, showing some understanding of Jewish religion and culture:

"Jews have a long history of being persecuted. They have a strong sense of family and friends. They believe they are chosen by God so they don't convert others."

Answers indicating accurate historical knowledge:

- "The Old Testament of the Bible is originated from Jewish history."

- "Jewish history is so long that it dated back to the stage before Christ."

- "The Jews have a festival called *Hanukkah* and Jerusalem is the Holy City for them."

- "Originally Hebrew people, David built a great kingdom, ran and protected her against foreign invasion. Prophets are important to a Jewish country."

- "Jewish God is very seriously worshipped."

- "I acquired some knowledge of history from the Bible; I know that in ancient days they acquired the land of Palestine and were driven off and after WWII they sought to reestablish their state. But I know little of their culture and history."

- "I learnt about Jewish history from Bible. And I had read a book titled 'The Great Jewish People.' From which I learnt about their paying special attention to education and there are lots of great thinkers and scientists and philosophers in its history."

- "It is said that the Jewish people pay attention to their children's education. If you have knowledge you can gain everything in the world."

- "Jews used to live in Jerusalem thousands of years ago. But later they were expelled. So they scattered all over the world today. However, they gathered again in Jerusalem and rebuilt a nation Israel. It's a miracle. I think their religion is Judaism."

- "Jewish people are originally from the Middle East. They have been oppressed many times in history by countries including: Egypt, Roman Empire, Germany (Nazis)."
- "The ancestors of the Jews are Hebrew who once lived in today's Middle East. Before the second century BC, and then they left. Israel was founded in 1948. They attach great importance to knowledge so they seem very smart."
- "History: very long, going back to 2000BC. Culture: Jewish culture exerts a great influence over the western culture. Jewish Bible has become an important part of the Christian Bible. Both Christianity and Islam have grown out of Jewish religion. Religion: Judaism."
- "Jewish have a suffering and misery history. They were the people who were always expelled and blamed such as the famous Diaspora history."
- "The Wailing Wall."
- "Jewish religion asks its affiliates to believe in their solely God."
- "The Jews is the first one thought there is only one God in the world."
- "Because of some religious beliefs and the death of Jesus, they were seen as enemy by some religions."
- "Jewish people had initiated the Christian religion."
- "They believe in Jehovah."
- "Jews and Christians worship the same God."
- "I think they do have a closest relationship with God as God was invented by them. Its not a joke."
- Nine students mentioned Einstein, two Karl Marx, one Kissinger, one Moses, and one — Beethoven!

Answers containing major errors:

- "They believe in Jesus."
- "They have own's religion, maybe it is Christianism."
- "Religion: Christ."
- "Jewish is originated in Europe."
- "Most of them believe in Islam."
- "Jewish history is very miserable. Jewish culture once was [in?]dependent but as far as I know there are no obvious differences from his partners of the Western World because of the economic globalization."
- "Jewish culture dated from the Bible. The God's son Jesus promised the Jews for their affluent land, which was called the desirous settlement."
- "I know that they once had been destroyed seriously by American White. About culture I know that there is a Jewish religion version of the Bible, they worshipped many different Gods."

Conclusion:

The students clearly know few details of the Jewish religion. Notably, fifty-seven students replied "I don't know," or gave equivalent replies. However, what the students do know, no matter how obvious to a Western, particularly Jewish person, is outstanding, given their limited resources and contact with Jewish people. It is significant that some students understand that Jews originated in the Middle East in current-day Israel, because this is the historical foundation of the Jewish people's claim to Israel. The overwhelming majority of students who attempted to answer the question replied with the Chinese stereotype that the Jews are "clever" and "good at business." One applicant even reported that there is research proving that Jews are the "cleverest race in the world." With obvious pride, several applicants drew comparisons between the characteristics of Jews and Chinese. Although the responses show very little detailed knowledge, they express a deep respect for Jews as a people and sympathy for its "miserable" history. Some students had heard that Jews place a high value on education. The responses clearly preferred to define the Jewish people's characteristics and historical legacy rather than give an analysis of Judaism. The lack of knowledge or apparent interest in religion is understandable, given that most students do not have a religion. China is an atheist country. But sources on Judaism are becoming available, and interest is growing in Chinese society.

Question 2:
What/who are your sources of knowledge of Jewish people?

Most students named more than one source. Overlap or combinations of sources are not indicated here.

1. TV: 46
2. Movies: 49
3. Books: 125[84]
4. Teachers: 30[85]
5. Other people: 21[86]
6. Bible: 20
7. Internet: 18
8. Newspaper: 18
9. Radio: 7
10. Magazines: 15

Conclusion:

The majority of students acquired their knowledge from books, which include history textbooks, paragraphs in English books, religion and culture class books, and novels. The Chinese culture has always valued literature, and with the recent liberalization of Chinese society, it is not surprising that many sources have become available. However, the information contained in these sources mainly provides information on famous Jewish intellectuals and Jewish suffering during the *Shoah*. It is somewhat surprising that teachers were mentioned only in thirty responses, but it is probable that many students who responded "books" were given or assigned these books by teachers. It is unclear how teachers presented Jews in their discussions. Movies and TV got a similar number of mentions. Many students named *The Pianist*, *Schindler's List*, and *Life is Beautiful* as movies they saw. Chinese students enjoy watching foreign films, and American films are more popular than European films, which reflects Chinese college students' intense interest in learning English, and in American culture.

Forty-six students reported that their source of information was TV. One student mentioned "the teaching programs on TV like *Discovery*" as his source of knowledge. It can be assumed that most of the TV programs were documentaries that contained information on the Jewish experience in World War II. Most of these students must have seen these programs before they came to college, since most Chinese college students do not have TVs. They rather watch DVDs or VCDs on their computers. Still, TV is an increasingly important source of information because the number of TV sets continues to grow. The Chinese fondness of educational TV makes teaching programs a very effective means of transmitting knowledge.

Significantly, twenty students reported the Bible as their source of knowledge for the Jewish people, while only three reported that they are Christian and two that they are Moslem. The Bible has become a requirement in some European culture and religion classes. The number of students reading the Bible may be a little high for university students, perhaps because these students are reading the Bible as part of the English language curriculum. However, since Christianity is said to be the fastest-growing religion in China, reading the Bible will become more popular for converts and atheists alike.

The Internet is the newest medium available to society, and it has clearly replaced the radio. It is significant that only seven people reported the radio as their source of information. Until the reform era, Chinese society relied on the radio for information. This survey shows that the radio is quickly becoming obsolete. Newspapers are for these students as popular as the Internet, though less popular than TV as a source on Jewish issues. A survey of how many college students regularly read newspapers, and how extensively Jewish issues are covered there would be necessary before more far-reaching conclusions about the role of newspapers could be drawn. Magazines are becoming another source, particularly of information for the young. However, it is unclear which magazines are read and what they cover.

Question 3:
What do you know about the history of Jews in China?

The following responses indicate where the students thought Jews have lived in China. Mentions of Shanghai and He Fang Shan were always linked to WWII.

1. Don't know: 145
2. Shanghai/WWII immigration: 31
3. Kaifeng: 8
   i. "In Henan Province of China there are some Jews. I know this from a book concerning Jewish culture."
   ii. "Most Jewish people are living in Kaifeng. Kaifeng is the biggest residence for Jews in China."
   iii. "In Kaifeng, Henan province, there is a group of people called themselves as descendents of Jewish. In Song Dynasty Jewish people settled down at Kaifeng and were respected by local government."
4. Song Dynasty: 1
   "It is said that there used to be a tribe of Jews arriving in China in the Song Dynasty. As a result of intermarriage, nowadays we can find no trace of them."
5. He Fang Shan: 1
   "In WWII a Chinese man called He Fang Shan saved lots of Jewish people, some of

which lived permanently in China since then."

6. Sui Dynasty: 1
   "They came to China before Sui dynasty and then stayed there."

7. Guizhou: 1
   "I'm not very familiar with the history of Jews in China. But I know there are also some Jews in China living in some remote areas in China such as Guizhou province."

8. Mr. Limadou: 1
   "Western people came to China hundreds of years ago and at the same time brought in the religion. Mr. Limadou first brought Jews to China."

9. Tang Dynasty: 3
   i. "It is said that the first Jews came to China in Tang dynasty. They did business with Chinese and preached their beliefs."
   ii. "Since the Tang dynasty they came to China."
   iii. "In Tang dynasty of China, maybe Xi'an, Chang'an called at that time."

10. 1840s first immigration: 1
    "In 1840s Jews first came to China."

11. Yuan Dynasty: 1
    "They came in the Yuan dynasty."

12. Dang Dynasty: 1
    "I guess in Dang Dynasty of China it was possible for Jews to travel to China, for in that time Zhang city, the capital of Dang Dynasty, was the commercial center of the world."

13. Shandong: 1
    "There seem to be a village which is built by Jewish long time ago in Shandong Province."

14. Shanxi: 1
    "I know there are some Jew in Shanxi province."

Conclusion:

The overwhelming majority of students could not answer this question, or their answers displayed a high degree of confusion both about Jewish residents in China and Chinese history. The history of Jews in China before World War II was one of small settlements that remained isolated and little known. The thirty-one responses showing knowledge of the Shanghai experience are accurate because the Chinese know a lot of details about World War II in China. The Chinese continue to feel proud that they helped rescue Jews during the war. It may be assumed that several of the students who gave correct answers came themselves from Shanghai or areas near Shanghai.

Question 4:
What do you know about the Jewish experience during WWII? Where did you learn about this experience?

The overwhelming majority of Chinese college students (188 of 214) have been exposed to the history of the *Shoah* through a variety of sources.

1. Books: 117
2. Movies: 80
3. TV: 26
4. Teachers: 22
5. Magazines: 7

6. Newspapers: 5
7. Heard from other people: 5
8. Internet: 4
9. Visited Nazi sites in Nuremberg, Germany: 1
10. He Ping Restaurant: 1: [87]

Conclusion:

These college students have learned much about the Jews' tragic experience during World War II. The replies ranged from simple answers to detailed and emotional explanations. Every response was sympathetic to the Jews. However, two students used this opportunity to express their dissatisfaction with Ariel Sharon's policies. If these data are compared to the data collected for Question 2, some interesting conclusions can be drawn. Respondents to both Question 2 and Question 4 reported in similar numbers that they learned about Jews from books; however, in response to Question 2, mostly textbooks were mentioned, whereas several references to literature were included in the responses to Question 4. The role of movies leads to an even more interesting comparison. Only forty-nine students replied to Question 2 that they saw movies on Jewish issues, while eighty replied to Question 4 that they had seen films about the *Shoah* It must have been the mention of World War II in Question 4 that caused thirty-one more students to recall that they did indeed see films about the Jews during the war. Foreign films gave the students a visual understanding of the *Shoah* that was lacking in responses solely based on books. These films have been the strongest basis of Chinese knowledge and emotional feelings about the *Shoah*. Several students equated the Chinese experience under Japanese occupation with the Jewish experience in Europe. One student mentioned the term "The Final Solution." Although the students knew about the Jewish tragedy, they did not understand the historical context in Europe that facilitated the *Shoah*. They held only Germany responsible. There was no knowledge of other European nations' participation in or indirect responsibility for the crimes. However, one student, showing more historic knowledge, responded, "They were killed by the Germans in the concentration camps. Other countries, even America and Canada, had refused to help them. The Christian and the Jews should be united and make peace. No race discrimination." Two students also reported reading Anne Frank's story in *The Diary of a Young Girl*.

Question 5:
What role do you think Jews play in modern Chinese society?

These Chinese students had never encountered a Jew in China and did not know that a small number of foreign Jews are living in China. Therefore, the answer that best sums up the majority view was a question: "There are Jews in China?"

1. Don't know: 112
2. No role: 23
3. Business/Technology: 20
4. Politics: 11
5. Same as all other foreigners: 8
6. Very important: 7
7. Culture: 3
8. Same as Chinese: 2
9. Pitied for WWII: 2

10. Education: 1
11. Auxiliary role: 1

Conclusion:

Considering that the students have no direct personal or even indirect knowledge about Jews living in China, it is incredible that twenty of them assert that Jews play an important role in Chinese business and technology and seven of them even believe that Jews are "very important." This coincides with the general Chinese belief that all Jews are "clever and good at business." Eleven students had some interesting political comments, for example, on Kissinger's role in improving Sino-American relations, the Jewish role in American politics, and Israel's contributions to the Chinese military. One student reported, "The relationship between China and Israel is OK." Another seemed upset that "last time Israel refused to sell pre-warning planes to China under American impression." Another student alludes to government control of information: "I think we didn't have a lot of cooperation's and the Chinese government didn't say much about Jews." Nine students mentioned that Jews and Chinese should be "friends." Nobody offered harsh criticism of Jewish people or provided negative stereotypes. No negative historic memories came to light.

Question 6:
What role do you think Jews play in the world?

When asked what role the Jews play in the world, without mentioning politics, the replies conform to widespread stereotypes:

1. Business/ Economics: 51
2. Don't know: 37
3. Generally important: 30
4. Science/Technology: 29
5. Politics (a role, but not a negative one): 27
6. Negative impression because of politics: 21
7. Same as others: 10
8. Not important: 7

Conclusion:

Chinese students believe that Jews play a significant role in the world's economic and scientific development. One student summarizes the collective response: "The Jews play a very important part in the world and they are the most clever people in the world. They accelerate the progress of the world politically, economically, culture, scientifically and so forth. Aiinstan [Einstein], Auerblart [?], Kixinge [Kissinger], Shalom [?] are the outstanding examples." However, the negative political responses to this question were often very strong: "Jews is aggressive and I think they cause many wars." One student offered a more positive and diplomatic statement: "I really feel grief whenever I hear the bombings in Israel. It's the killings between human beings. Yet the conflict is hard to resolve. We only hope one day peace will come. With the brilliance of the Jews, they can make it." Thus, although there was significant outrage against Israeli policies, the majority of students chose to answer this question by emphasizing the positive contributions of the Jews to the world. The number of students commenting on politics in a neutral or pro-Jewish manner slightly outnumbered the negative responses. However, the next question addressed politics more directly, stimulating some harsher replies.

Question 7:
Do you separate Israeli politics from the Jewish people, why or why not?

Summarizing the responses to this question proved somewhat problematic. Some responses were illogical or irrelevant, and others unclear, due to misunderstandings regarding the definition of "Israeli" and "Jewish". The following results are noteworthy:

1. "No, because Israel represents all Jews": 42
2. "No, because Jews always support their government": 2
3. "No," for a variety of reasons, mostly unclear: 26
4. "Yes, a government and its people are separate": 22
5. "Yes," for various unclear reasons: 6
6. "Yes, not all Israelis are Jewish": 2
7. "Yes, people cannot be blamed for inevitable political situations" — no hostility towards Israel: 2
8. Don't know: 87

Conclusion:
About half of the students who responded were not sure or had no opinion. Most students who do not separate between Israeli politics and the Jewish people expressed some variation of the following opinion: "I basically do not. The reason is simple. Israeli is a nation that composes merely of Jewish people." Some students were much more hostile to Israeli policy, stating, "No I don't as a matter of fact. I think lots of peace problems have a quite close relationship with the Jewish people." Another "No" response, but without rational justification, was: "Not really, I don't know, it just comes up to me like that."

Surprisingly, only twenty-two students said that they made a clear distinction because "a government and its people are separate." The Chinese usually make clear distinctions between governments and their people, but in this case, the students probably considered the overwhelming majority of Jews as a completely united people, and therefore did not differentiate between the Israeli government and the Jewish people, as they would have done for other countries.

One student did differentiate: "Yes because in my opinion Israeli politics, especially the current Israeli politics under Sharon government, is those politicians game. Every ordinary Jew wishes a peaceful life." Thus, the government and the people are not the same; the government is somehow evil but the Jews retain their image as a peaceful and historically victimized people. One particularly emotional student wrote, "No, we [do not] understand these killings, in both ethnic groups. A RESPONSIBLE government shouldn't let this happen, whatever their claims are." A few students felt that the American role in Israeli politics was to blame for the current situation.

One student indicates how some Chinese get their information: "They [the Israeli government and the Jewish people] are the same, I got the idea in the newspaper." The official Chinese bias emerges clearly in such responses. The Chinese press relies only on government information and is not allowed to offer perspectives that differ from the official one. The public media shape public opinion. It is more surprising that so many other students replied, "I don't know," instead of offering the politically correct standard view. In fact, few listed newspapers as their primary source of knowledge for Jews and Israel. It would be interesting to know what percentage of college students are reading international news to follow the Middle East crisis. Considering that China and Israel did not establish diplomatic relations until 1991, the students' knowledge of and sympathy for Israelis (though not the Israeli government) are formidable. The most thoughtful, though not conclusive response was: "Yes, Israeli politics is partly controlled by the US. But the conflicts in the Middle East are much more complicated. Concerning historical and cultural problems." This student addresses the complexity of the question, which his/her peers might have found too difficult to articulate.

Question 8:
Is there anything you would like to know more about Judaism as a culture or religion?

The responses were overwhelmingly enthusiastic and curious. Most students expressed further interest.

1. Yes, with enthusiasm: 107
2. Insults: 3
   i. "I really want to know if Jews are aliens which was sended to earth by God from other planet."
   ii. "Why don't they die out?" [Known as a Moslem extremist].
   iii. "I'd like to say something. I used to consider the Jewish people as clever, peacelike and pay lots of attention to their sufferings during WWII. Under the current circumstances, I changed my view and I opposite to them about they have done and what they are doing now on Arabic people. The Jews behavior interprets their arrogance and aggression."
3. No: 21
4. Don't know: 27

Topics students are interested in:

1. Education: "In my opinion this is vital reason for Jewish people to be superior to others." Many students are interested in Jewish education. Young Chinese are becoming more critical of their own education system.
2. "Why there is war between Israel and Palestine?" They want to know the history of both peoples and all other relevant, objective information.
3. Many expressed an interest in learning about Jewish culture, traditions, and daily life.
4. Some students want to understand the religion better, asking for a clear summary of the main Jewish beliefs. Some would like to know the difference between Judaism and Christianity. "So Jews believe in Christianity to some extent?"
5. One student poses three questions: "a. Why are they so successful in the Congress's aisle? [U.S. politics]. b. Why the U.S. Jews deserted the Euro Jews in the WWII and let them suffer? c. Are the Jewish people satisfied with their current achievement in the world?"
6. "What do synagogues look like?" Chinese have never been in a synagogue, and the Jewish religion is often described as "mysterious".

7. The history of Judaism and how it influenced other people.
8. "Do all Jews believe in Judaism?" "Do all Jews believe in God?"
9. "What is unique about Judaism?"
10. They want to know why Jewish people are successful, wise, clever, and good at business.
11. Some simply responded, "Since I don't know anything, I want to know everything!"
12. "What are Jewish people like now?"
13. "Actually, I know little about Judaism, but I'm not interested in it. Since your questions aroused my interest so I'd like to know everything connected with Judaism."
14. "Are Jews still discriminated against today?"
15. "The similarity and difference between Shanghai people and them."
16. Several students want to know "what their future is."
17. One student would "like to know a Jew and even make friends with him or her."
18. "I want to know what Israeli people and Palestine people feel about Sharon's words and actions now. I hope Israeli people and Palestine people know more about each other and become friends rather than enemies as soon as possible."
19. A student's advice to the Jews: "In my eyes Judaism is very mysterious religion. But most people don't know it very well. Maybe Jews should do more propaganda!"
20. "Culture! I know little. Would you like to tell us in English corner next time?"
21. Several women would like to know the role of women in Jewish religion. They are concerned about gender discrimination.
22. "Distributed over the world, what is the cohesion between Jews holding them together?"
23. One student would like to know about Jewish music and arts.
24. "I wish that I could understand how Judaism taught its people to be faithful to families and self-conscious."
25. One male bought a book about famous Jewish people and plans to read it over the Chinese New Year. He is eager to "learn everything."
26. A response that summarizes the desire of many students, constrained by a lack of resources: "Very much [would I like to know], but I don't have the resources."
27. "How do they think of German and other people in the world?"
28. "Why do Judaists have to receive the circumcision as their signal of their identity? Why not choose something noticeable and unpainful eg tattoo?"
29. "I want to know something about Jews in China."

4. Final Conclusion

The responses are overwhelmingly positive and inquisitive, taking into consideration that Chinese students are isolated from Jewish culture and religion. Although there were inevitable linguistic misunderstandings, nine out of ten students communicated very well. These

Chinese students did well by international comparison. If similar questions about Chinese history, politics, culture, and World War II experience would be submitted to American college students, the responses would not be more sophisticated. Chinese college students are making great efforts to understand the outside world, with a particular interest in American and other Western cultures. The Chinese see the Jews as a very special and interesting part of the West. Young Chinese people will be overwhelmingly receptive to more information about Israel, the Jewish people, and Judaism.

ANNEX 4. Sources

Four main sources provided the basis for this report:

- Articles and books by Chinese, Jewish, and other scholars, published over the last twenty or more years, that deal with Sino-Judaic relations and the history of Jews in China; professional literature on Chinese history and culture, and more specialized publications on current Chinese problems and policy issues. Many of the written sources used are mentioned in the footnotes.

- Close to one hundred personal interviews with Chinese and Jewish (mainly Israeli and American) scholars, experts, and policy advisors, carried out mainly between November 2002 and November 2003, although contacts were maintained with some of them until October 2004. In China, interviews were conducted at academic study centers specializing in Jewish studies, the Middle East, or international relations, in Beijing, Tianjin, Kaifeng, Jinan, Kunming, Shanghai, and Nanjing, where the majority of relevant centers can be found. In addition, religious leaders, diplomats, and media persons were consulted. Jewish sinologists provided help and information, in Israel at the universities of Jerusalem, Tel Aviv, and Haifa, and in the United States at Harvard, Princeton, Ann Arbor, Stanford, Wesleyan, and the State University of West Georgia. Jewish policy makers, diplomats, and experts with business links to China were also interviewed. Additional interviews were conducted with experts from Australia, France, Germany, and the United Kingdom. The acknowledgements in Annex 5 give their names in alphabetic order.

- Question-and-answer sessions with young Chinese students of Jewish culture and history, or other fields, in six universities in different parts of China (Beijing, Shanghai, Nanjing, Kaifeng, Jinan, and Kunming). These sessions were organized in October and November 2003 for the purpose of this report. Annex 1 quotes most of the questions asked.

- A written survey designed and carried out from October to December 2003 by Lauren Katz, an American student in Beijing, on Beijing college students' understanding of Judaism. Annex 3 provides an extensive summary of the results.

ANNEX 5. Acknowledgements

A large number of scholars, experts, policy makers, and businessmen in China, Israel, the United States, and other countries have helped the author to write this report. Between November 2002 and October 2004, many made helpful suggestions and exposed themselves to often lengthy interviews. Some helped to set up interviews with others or gave considerable time to discuss the report with the author. These few would deserve particular praise. If their names are not more emphasized, it is to avoid giving offense to others. Without the generous advice of all, this report would not have come to light. Even so, many shortcomings remain. For these, the author is alone responsible. But for the help he received, he owes thanks to the following persons:

Wendy Abraham, *Stanford, USA*; Robert E. Allinson, *Hong Kong*; Eliav Benjamin, *Shanghai*; Jan Berris, *New York, USA*; Rifka Bitterman, *Jerusalem*; Cao Jian, *Jerusalem*; Paul Cohen, *Cambridge, USA*; Ron Cohen, *Beijing*; Cong Cong, *Nanjing*; Paul Crook, *London*; Albert E. Dien, *Stanford, USA*; Irene Eber, *Jerusalem*; Israel Epstein, *Beijing*; Shimon Freundlich, *Beijing*; Fu Bo, *Beijing*; Fu You-de, *Jinan;* Gao Qiufu, *Beijing*; Shalom/Dina Greenberg, *Shanghai*; Sherwood Goldberg, *Washington D.C., USA*; Merle Goldman, *Cambridge, USA*; Jonathan Goldstein, *Carrollton, USA*; Gong Fang Zhen, *Shanghai*; Alfred Gottschalk, *Cincinatti, USA*; Antoine Halff, *Paris*; Malcolm I. Hoenlein, *New York, USA*; Hong Yinxing, *Nanjing*; Huang Fuwu, *Jinan*; Kenneth Jacobson, *New York, USA*; Jiansheng Zhang, *Kunming*; Jin Canrong, *Beijing*; Jin Ze, *Beijing*; Seth Kaplan, *New York, USA*; Lauren Katz, *Beijing/Washington D.C., USA;* Shlomi Kofman, *Jerusalem*; Peter Kupfer, *Mainz, Germany*; Isy Leibler, *Jerusalem*; Donald D. Leslie, *Canberra, Australia*; Dennis A. Leventhal, *Chestertown, USA*; Hillel Levine, *Cambridge, USA*; Li Li, *Tianjin*; Li Weijian, *Shanghai*; Liang Gong, *Kaifeng*; Kenneth Lieberthal, *Ann Arbor, USA*; Lin Zhen, *Beijing*; Roberta Lipson, *Beijing*; Liu Xinli, *Jinan*; Ly Ye, *Kunming*; Harriet Mandel, *New York, USA*; Daniel S. Mariaschin, *Washington D.C., USA*; Michel Masson s.j., *Paris*; Mei Junjie, *Shanghai*; Meng Jianhua, *Beijing*; Maisie J. Meyer, *London*; Miao Xian, *Beijing*; Harriet Mouchly-Weiss, *New York, USA*; Muhammed Sayed Ma Yun Fu, *Beijing*; Ni Shixiong, *Shanghai*; Pan Guang, *Shanghai*; Andrew Plaks, *Princeton, USA*; Michael Pollak, *Dallas, USA*; Eyal Propper, *Beijing*; Arthur H. Rosen, *Washington D.C., USA*; Walter Rosenbaum, *Paris/Konstanz*; Menachem

Schmelzer, *New York, USA*; Vera Schwarcz, *Middletown, USA*; Aron Shai, *Tel Aviv*; Yitzhak Shelef, *Jerusalem*; Yitzhak Shichor, *Haifa*; Richard A. Siegel, *New York, USA*; Elyse Beth Silverberg, *Beijing*; Georgia Smith, *Paris*; Suolao Wang, *Beijing*; Henry Tang, *New York, USA*; Marvin Tokayer, *Great Neck, USA*; Noam Urbach, *Beer-Sheva*; Jean-Jacques Wahl, *Paris*; Wang Dehua, *Shanghai*; Wang Haoqiang, *Beijing*; Wang Jian, *Shanghai*; Wang Jianping, *Shanghai*; Wang Lixin, *Tianjin*; Wang Xiaoli, *Beijing*; Wang Xiaoshu, *Shanghai*; Wang Yu, *Beijing*; Wei Naxin, *Mainz, Germany*; Weiming Zhao, *Shanghai*; Wu Lei, *Kunming*; Andrew Wyckoff, *Paris*; Xiao Xian, *Kunming*; Xu Ding Xin, *Nanjing*; Xu Feng, *Kunming*; Xu Xin, *Nanjing*; Xun Zhou, *London*; Michael Yahuda, *London*; Amnon Yaish, *Paris*; Yang Haijun, *Kaifeng*; Yang Jun, *Kunming*; Yin Gang, *Beijing*; Yu Jiafu, *Beijing*; Zhang Fan, *Beijing*; Zhang Ligang, *Kaifeng*; Zhang Ping, *Tel Aviv*; Zhang Qianhong, *Kaifeng*; Zheng Bangshan, *Kaifeng*; Zheng Qian, *Jinan*; Zhou Xiefan, *Beijing*; Zhu Weilie, *Shanghai*.

In addition, thanks are due to Ambassador Dennis Ross, Washington, Chairman of the Board of the Jewish People Policy Planning Institute, whose support and advice were very precious; to other members of the Board, and to Professor Yehezkel Dror, Jerusalem, Founding President of the Institute, whose guidance and attention to detail were indispensable. Thanks go to all colleagues of the Institute who had the kindness to read and comment on the report: Avinoam Bar-Yosef, Professor Sergio DellaPergola, Naftali Elimelech, Avi Gil, Sharon Pardo, Michael Weil, and Ahava Zarembski.

The planning of travels, visits, and interviews in Israel, the United States, and China was a complex and time-consuming task, flawlessly organized by several helpful persons. The overall coordination was maintained by Ms. Ita Alkalay from the Jewish People Policy Planning Institute in Jerusalem; she also set up the visits in Israel. The visits in the United States were organized by Ms. Adina Kay from the Consulate of Israel in New York, and those in China by Mr. Lu Jian from the Embassy of the People's Republic of China in Washington D.C., and Ms. Fu Bo and her staff from the Chinese Education Association for International Exchange in Beijing. Thanks are due to all of them.

Last but not least, I express my particular gratitude to my interpreter and friend Mr. Wang Haoqiang (Philip Wang) in Beijing, who accompanied me on my visits in China and helped me to better understand the complexity of his country and the subtlety of its culture, and to my former colleague Ms. Miriam Koreen in Paris, who helped to present the report in an acceptable form.

HISTORIC APPENDIX. Notes on Jewish Encounters with China across the Ages

1. THE FIRST TRACES: EARLY RABBINIC AND GAONIC TIMES

China must have appeared on the mental map of the Jewish people earlier than is generally believed. When exactly knowledge of China reached the Jews for the first time is shrouded in the mist of history. If it was not already in late biblical, it certainly was in early rabbinic times (first century B.C.E.–second century C.E.) when real contacts between China and West Asia started, and Jews participated actively in the civilization and economy of the Roman Empire and Persian-dominated Babylon. Both Romans and Persians knew of China because they loved silk. Trade in Chinese silk was indirect, and much of it was rewoven in Middle Eastern workshops. From early rabbinic, Talmudic, and Roman sources we learn that Jews were active as producers and traders of silk. The rabbinic literature has several words for silk and many references to it, which indicates the popularity and widespread use of the fabric among ancient Jews.[88] Jews must have heard of the famous land of silk, just as their Roman and Persian rulers and neighbors had. It has been suggested that *shirajin*, one of the Aramaic words in the Talmud for silk, and of unclear origin, may have a linguistic link with the Chinese word for silk, *si*.

There has been some speculation about when Jews first reached China. The Jews of Kaifeng claimed arrival at the time of the Han dynasty (206 B.C.E.–220 C.E.), which, if true, would coincide with the arrival of Jewish refugees in India following the destruction of the Second Temple in 70 C.E.. However, most historians propose later dates. Reliable sources and traces indicating a Jewish presence appear more or less simultaneously between the eighth and tenth centuries, when the Tang dynasty ruled China. Arab historians of that period (particularly Ibn-Kordâdbeh) mention the presence of Jews in a number of Chinese cities, and the important role the "Radanites" played–a then unique group of Jewish businessmen who transported merchandise (and scientific and technological knowledge) by land and sea all the way from Spain and France via the Middle East to China and back.

The current Hebrew word for China, *Sin,* or similar terms can be found for the first time in works of Jewish authors of this, the "Gaonic" period. One is Eldad Ha-Dani, a Hebrew author of fantastic travel tales who lived in the ninth century and pretended to have been kidnapped and moved to China — a story that no historian believes. More serious is the Karaite writer Al-Qirqisani, a contemporary of the greatest of the *Geonim*, Saadia Gaon (tenth century). He reported that the Babylonian reading of the Masoretic Bible text was valid for Jews up to the borders of China.[89] These casual references to China, both in a Jewish fairy tale and in a scholarly observation, indicate that the existence of China and the fact that Jews lived there or near to it, must have been known to Jewish writers of the time. In fact, two pages of text discovered in the early twentieth century in different places testify to the life or activity of Jews in Tang China. Both are on paper, which was then used only in China, and date back to the eighth or ninth century. One is a page of Hebrew prayers found in Dunhuang on the Chinese Silk Road. The pleas of this Jew, who prayed at the end of the known world with quotes from the Prophets and Psalms, strike a chord until this day:

> Gather Your dispersed people, cleanse the sins of Judah, give Your people a banner for rallying, oh Builder of Jerusalem...![90]

2. THE JEWS OF KAIFENG: TWELFTH TO NINETEENTH CENTURY

The early sources mentioned above do not prove cultural encounters. They indicate contacts or presence but not dialogue. Cultural encounters between Chinese and Jews, even a strong sense of spiritual affinity, appear for the first time in the written records of the Jews of Kaifeng.

No later than 1120, a small Jewish community, at least partly of Persian origin, flourished in Kaifeng, in the Henan province, the imperial capital of the Northern Song dynasty (960-1127). In the following centuries, learned members of this community engraved texts on stone that emphasized close similarities between traditional Chinese-Confucian and Jewish beliefs and practices. The community placed a number of these stone stelae, dated 1489, 1512, 1663, and 1679 in its synagogue and other places. The stone texts, which are unique in Jewish history, were read and reported by French Jesuit missionaries of the seventeenth and eighteenth centuries. They were published in complete English translation for the first time only in 1942, by Bishop White of the Canadian Church of England.

The earliest stone, dated 1489, presents Abraham as the founder of the Jewish religion and a firm opponent of idolatry. The 1512 inscription reinforces this message:

> They made no images, flattered no spirits and ghosts, and placed no credence in superstitious practices [1489] ... As to the modeling of statues and figures, and the painting of forms and colors, they are vain matters and empty practices [1512] ...[91]

These texts are in line both with rabbinic traditions that tell of Abraham's destruction of his father's stone idols, and with the philosophy of the Confucian elites that did not support the widespread popular idolatry of the Chinese. What these apologetic texts want to show is that Jews could easily find common ground with a China that was setting the cultural standards. We have no written Chinese reactions to these inscriptions, but may safely assume that official attitudes were friendly because the time from the late fifteenth to the seventeenth century, when the Ming dynasty ruled, was a "golden age" for the Jews. A small number of them passed the extremely demanding imperial examinations and reached high social status as civil and military officials. This was historically unique. In Christian and Moslem countries, and one exception in eleventh-century Spain, non-baptized Jews were strictly barred from senior careers and achievements in public, particularly military services, until the nineteenth or even twentieth century.

3. THE EUROPEAN ENLIGHTENMENT AGE: MENASSEH BEN ISRAEL AND BARUCH SPINOZA

Menasseh Ben Israel and Baruch Spinoza are the two epoch-making Jewish thinkers in the West who for the first time, looked at Jews in a Chinese context — or inversely, at the Chinese in a Jewish context. They remained alone among Jews and Chinese until the late eighteenth and nineteenth centuries. Probably neither of them had met any Chinese, whether Jews or non-Jews, and neither knew that the Jews of Kaifeng were just reaching the last apogee of their long history while they were writing their books in Amsterdam. Menasseh acquired his place of honor in Jewish history by his intervention with the Lord Protector of England Oliver Cromwell in 1655, to annul the expulsion of Jews from England that had been decreed in 1290. In preparation for his visit to London, Menasseh published in 1650 his *Esperança de Israel*, followed by the English version *Hope of Israel*. In this work he argued among other things that the existence of Jews in China, allegedly descendents of the legendary Ten Tribes, supported his claim that Jews should also be allowed to live in England.[92]

Baruch Spinoza was obviously interested in Jews, but not Chinese Jews, although he probably knew Menasseh personally and had read his books. In 1670, twenty years after Menasseh's *Esperança*, he published his famous, iconoclastic *Tractatus Theologico-Politicus*, in which he compared the fate of the Chinese and Jews in a long-term historic perspective:

> The mark of circumcision, too, I consider to be such an important factor in this matter that I am convinced that this by itself will preserve their nation forever. Indeed, were it not that the fundamental principles of their religion discourage manliness, I would not hesitate to believe that they will one day, given the opportunity — such is the mutability of human affairs — establish once more their independent state, and that God will again choose them. The Chinese afford us an outstanding example of that possibility. They, too, religiously observe the custom of the pigtail which sets them apart from all other people, and they have preserved themselves as a separate people for so many thousands of years that they far surpass all other nations in antiquity. They have not always maintained their independence, but they did regain it after losing it, and will no doubt recover it again when the spirit of the Tartars becomes enfeebled by reason of luxurious living and sloth.[93]

This comparison is extraordinary. Only after the birth of the new China and Israel in 1948–1949 was it possible to appreciate Spinoza's foresight. He understood that the world's two oldest continuous civilizations were likely to emerge one day from defeat and occupation and regain their independence, because both were so stubbornly maintaining their difference from others. Spinoza's emphasis on two external, physical signs of difference rather than cultural memory and language was ill conceived, but did not reduce the strength of his main argument. He was the first to understand that a similar law of history might apply to the Jews and the Chinese. Menasseh and Spinoza had no immediate Jewish or other followers who speculated about these two nations. Only in the later part of the nineteenth century did the Chinese and Jews discover each other as distinct cultures of historic significance, and only in the twentieth century did a genuine and sustained encounter between the two become possible.

4. MODERN JEWISH AWARENESS OF CHINA

How and when did modern Jewish awareness of China begin? The answer could show communalities between the two peoples and how Jews perceived these communalities a hundred or more years ago. But it is more difficult to answer this question than the question of how the Chinese perceived the Jews (Chapter 4.2). The difficulty stems from the wide geographic spread of the Jewish people and the many languages spoken and written by Jews, as well as the devastation suffered during World War II. Not only most of Europe's Jews, but also most of their cultural documents and their living memory have been destroyed. Towards the end of the nineteenth century, the most successful Jewish publications relating to China were about the Jews of China. Jewish visitors and writers paid new attention to the impoverished remnants of a once proud community, an interest that was part of a growing feeling of religious or national solidarity among Jewish leaders and intellectuals of the time. In 1900, Marcus Nathan Adler, son of a Chief Rabbi of the British Empire, delivered a speech in London on the Jews of China. It was immediately printed and in 1909, a scholar-merchant, S. M. Perlman, published a paper "The Jews in China." Both authors were focusing on the Kaifeng Jews, but they were not parochial. They had an interest in the context, in China's culture and history, and made comparisons. Adler said:

> The Chinese and the Jews belong to the oldest nations in the world, but whilst the Chinese are the most isolated and self-contained of peoples, it may be said that the Jews are the most widespread and scattered.[94]

Perlman emphasized — perhaps the first Jewish author to do so — the absence of discrimination against Jews in old China, in stark contrast to the Christian West. His comparison represented a Jewish exception from the general contempt of China displayed by European imperialists during their heyday. In 1911, Perlman published *Ha-Sinim* ("The Chinese") in modern Hebrew — almost certainly the first history of China to appear in the still-developing old-new language of the Jewish people.[95] The extraordinary reception of Adler's and Perlman's papers by the Jewish world is significant. Adler's was immediately translated into German, Russian, and Hebrew; Perlman's into Russian and Hebrew, and both were several times reprinted in English in abridged or enlarged editions. They were thus made accessible to the overwhelming majority of the Jewish people. This testified to a beginning enthusiasm in the Jewish world for China and Chinese Jews, an interest that would soon be constrained if not extinguished by the more pressing priorities of helping Jewish refugees from Russia, the Zionist program, and later on, the turmoil of the two World Wars.

A big and still unexplored issue is the literature on China that was written during the period of 1900 to 1939 in Yiddish.[96] The first known Yiddish reference to China goes back to 1788, when a fairy tale about a Chinese princess who married a fisherman was published in Germany. Several popular Yiddish books about China appeared before and after World War I. One, *Chinese Philosophy and Poetry*, by A. Almi (1925), is a scholarly work. The author scolds his people in lively Yiddish for a perceived lack of interest in China, in terms that could still be applied to a number of Jews today:

> Often I heard the strange argument "Why suddenly the Chinese? Write about Jews!" As if the whole wide world, the Chinese or even the Tatars [?], were of no concern to us at all. Such arguments smack of complacency and provincialism. We have built a "Jewish Wall of China" around ourselves. At best, we will occasionally go to smell the air of Berlin or Paris, but this is already the end of our world. "What — China, India? You must be completely crazy"![97]

Another thread of Jewish receptivity for China that has barely been explored is enthusiasm for Chinese art, the most popular expression of China's culture. At the turn of the nineteenth century, the donations of German Jews were indispensable in creating Germany's public collections of East Asian art; Jews made the overwhelming majority of East Asian art donations. Until approximately 1914, no public German money was available for Chinese art. The director of Germany's Imperial Museums complained in a letter of 1909 about his Emperor Wilhelm II: "His aversion against the yellow race [*sic*] applies, alas, to their art as well!"[98] It is Jews who held high the glory of China's art against his Imperial Majesty's racist aversions. At the first comprehensive exhibition of Chinese art to take place in Europe, that of Berlin in 1929, a large proportion of all 1,272 objects on display belonged to collectors with obviously Jewish names.[99] Since then or in parallel, Jews in several other countries, particularly the United States, and also in France, formed collections of Chinese art. The Jews of Israel too have shown their affection for China — during the exceptional Chinese art exhibition held by the Israel Museum in Jerusalem in 2001.[100] Maybe Jews sense a particular affinity here, based on the quality of an art that emphasizes the abstract beauty of color and form and the "Soundless Poetry"[101] of landscape more than the human body, an art that also contains no Christian references or symbols.

In German-speaking countries, the impact of Chinese philosophy and culture on Jews went widely beyond art. The philosopher Martin Buber introduced Daoism from 1910 on to the Jewish reading public and to a much larger German audience. His interpretations and translations, made with the help of a Chinese scholar, were very popular. After his emigration to Israel in 1938, he produced the first modern Hebrew translation of Daoism's main text, the *Daodejing* of Laozi. After the Kaifeng Jews' search for religious affinities between Confucianism and Judaism in the fifteenth and sixteenth centuries, Martin Buber represents so far the most influential Jewish effort to find common religious-philosophical ground between Jewish thought and the thought of ancient China. But his interest was in Daoism, probably more than Confucianism. In Daoist scriptures and legends, Buber saw parallels to Hasidism, the mystical movement that sprang up among East European Jews in the eighteenth century. What fascinated the Jewish philosopher in both mystical cultures was the meeting of natural and supernatural events, of the divine and the human, in mundane, daily life, as if the natural and the supernatural were both self-evident.

In the decades following World War II, the contributions of Jewish sinologists started to have an impact on Western research and intellectual appreciation of China. In less than two generations since the beginning of the century, Jewish historians had turned from authors of brochures on a forgotten community and a remote empire into world-class China scholars. Jews became prominent in sinology as in other academic fields, but some of them applied perspectives and concerns born in their own Jewish origin, to the study of China's past and present.

Chinese and Jews are ancient civilizations, which have struggled to modernize while retaining some of the essential sources of their own tradition. The communality of this historic challenge has fascinated and preoccupied the great American sinologist Joseph Levenson. His *Confucian China and its Modern Fate — The Problem of Intellectual Continuity* of the late 1950s and his following works have dominated many sinological discussions for a generation. Equally influential was the later work of the great Harvard scholar Benjamin Schwartz, particularly his monumental book *The World of Thought in Ancient China* (1985). Both Levenson and Schwartz have admitted that their profound interest in modern China's relationship with its ancient cultural heritage was intimately linked to their concern with their own Jewish past. In an essay by Schwartz that eulogized his friend Levenson who had died prematurely, he alluded to his and Levenson's Jewishness as a key reason for their deep empathy with China:

> His interest in the relationship of modern Chinese to their cultural heritage was intimately tied to his undisguised concern with his own Jewish past. It is a concern which I share with him and which made me feel very close to him. Far from impairing his objectivity, it seems to me that it lent an honesty and authenticity to his thought which is not readily found in the writing of many supposedly objective scholars who vainly fancy that they are leaving themselves outside of their work.[102]

Sinologists of Jewish origin have challenged other hackneyed ideas. Paul Cohen, a student and colleague of Schwartz in Harvard, published in 1984 his *Discovering History in China*, in which he attacked the "intellectual imperialism of American historians" of China and their "Western-centeredness."[103] Needless to say, the translation of Cohen's book was a best-seller in China, and Chinese scholars alluded to Cohen's Jewish origin as a likely reason for his ability to distance himself from majority views on China and propose new and original ideas. It will come as no surprise that other scholars have given their attention to ancient Chinese literature and poetry, the history of Islam in China, China's modern intellectual history, the evolution of post-Mao China, human rights, the fate of Chinese dissidents, the Chinese military, and other contemporary issues.

At the same time, Jewish historians have also focused research on the old documents that have survived from the community in Kaifeng, or on the history of Jews in twentieth-century Shanghai and Harbin. These scholars wanted to explore the actual historical encounters between Chinese and Jews. They approached the question of communalities between these two civilizations through the relations and the shared experiences of real people.

Will there be a new generation of equally committed Jewish China scholars? The answer will be of more than academic interest. It could influence future intellectual encounters between Chinese and Jews, as well as their mutual understanding and appreciation.

NOTES

1. Reported by *China Industrial and Commercial Times* and repeated by one of the leading Internet search engines, www.sina.com (dated 23 June 2004).
2. See www.hkjewishfilmfest.org
3. James F. Hoge, "A Global Power Shift in the Making — Is the United States Ready?", *Foreign Affairs*, July/August 2004, p. 2.
4. Evan S. Medeiros and M. Taylor Fravel, "China's New Diplomacy", *Foreign Affairs*, November/December 2003, p. 32.
5. Avraham Altman and Irene Eber, "Flight to Shanghai 1938-1940: The Larger Setting", *Yad Vashem Studies XXVIII*, Jerusalem, 2000, p. 53.
6. W. J. Peterson, A. H. Plaks, et al., eds., *The Power of Culture — Studies in Chinese Cultural History*, Hong Kong, 1994, Introduction.
7. John King Fairbank and Merle Goldman, *China — A New History*, enlarged edition, Cambridge, MA/London, 1998, p. 18.
8. Pierre Ryckmans, "The Chinese Attitude towards the Past", *Papers on Far Eastern History 39*, Canberra: The Australian National University, Department of Far Eastern History, March 1989, pp. 1, 2, 7, 13, footnote 1.
9. Martin Schaaper, *An Emerging Knowledge-Based Economy in China? Indicators From OECD Databases.* Organization for Economic Co-operation and Development, DSTI/DOC (2004) 4, 22 March 2004.
10. John Vinocur, "A European Doomsday Scenario — French Research Group Paints a Gloomy Economic Picture", *New York Herald Tribune*, 14 May 2003.
11. *China in the World Economy — The Domestic Policy Challenges*, Organization for Economic Co-operation and Development, Paris, 2002.
12. Schaaper, op.cit., pp. 52-57.
13. Mu-ming Poo, "Cultural reflections", and seven other contributions by Chinese and American-Chinese scientists, in "China-Messages to China from the West", Supplement to *Nature — International Weekly Journal of Science*, 11 March 2004, pp. 203-222.

    These articles were first published in Chinese at the end of 2003.
14. Fairbank-Goldman, op.cit., p.1.
15. Orville Schell, "China's Hidden Democratic Legacy", *Foreign Affairs*, July/August 2004, p. 117.
16. Figures and projections of this subchapter were reviewed by Mr. Antoine Halff, Oil Industry and Markets Division, IEA (International Energy Agency), Paris.
17. *Oil Market Report*, International Energy Agency Paris, 13 November 2003, pp. 4-9; "China's Growing Thirst for Oil Remakes the Global Market", *The Wall Street Journal Online*, 3 December 2003, pp. 1-5.
18. These data, provided by the International Energy Agency (IEA), Paris, are approximate.
19. Nawaf E. Obaid et al., *The Sino-Saudi Energy Rapprochement: Implications for US National Security*, The Gracia Group, Prepared for the Office of Secretary of Defense, Department of Defense, Washington D.C., 8 January 2002; "Sino-Saudi Crude Trade Expands", *Petroleum Argus*, Vol. XXXIII, 48, 8 December 2003.
20. Wu Lei, "East Asian Energy Security and Middle East Oil", *Middle East Economic Survey*, Vol. XLV, No. 48, 2 December 2002, pp. D2-D6.

    This article, which appeared also in Chinese, was commended by senior Chinese policy makers.

21 "China, Korea and Japan plan to establish a unified energy market", *China Petroleum Report*, No. 47, Beijing, 27 November 2003, pp.1-2.

22 Prof. Wang Lixin, Nankai University, Tianjin, interview of 30 October 2003.

23 Donald D. Leslie, *Jews and Judaism in Traditional China — A Comprehensive Bibliography*, Monumenta Serica Monograph Series, Sankt Augustin, Nettetal, 1998, pp. 49-51. On Arab historians see also Historic Appendix, section 1.

24 Wang Tai Peng, "Islam in China", *AsianEye, Asia Inc*, April 2004, p. 11.

Wang mentions the appointment of thirty registered female [sic] imams in Ningxia province, which he recommends as one of the "more enlightened things that Arab Islamic fundamentalist countries can learn from China"!

25 *Statement by the Acting Assistant Professor, Religious Studies, Stanford University, Dr. Jacqueline Armijo to the Congressional-Executive Commission on China*, 24 July 2003. www.cecc.gov/pages/hearings/072403/armijo.php. pp. 1-6.

26 *The Sino-Saudi Energy Rapprochement*, op.cit., p.36.

27 Bernard Lewis, *The Crisis of Islam — Holy War and Unholy Terror*, New York, 2003, p. 164.

28 Dru C. Gladney, *Dislocating China — Muslims, Minorities and Other Subaltern Subjects*, London, 2004, pp. 312-335.

29 *Islam in China*, English and Chinese, Beijing, no date.

30 Bernard Lewis, op.cit., p. 92.

31 George J. Gilboy, "The Myth Behind China's Miracle", *Foreign Affairs*, July/August 2004, pp. 33, 35, 37.

32 This is a private, non-profit organization pursuing the study and preservation of Jewish history in China, and supporting Chinese scholarship in Judaism as well as translations and exhibitions. Every few months, the institute publishes a newsletter, *Points East*.

33 *American Attitudes Toward Chinese Americans and Asian Americans*, A "Committee of 100" Survey, Committee of 100, New York, 2001, pp. 8, 11, 13.

34 Vera Schwarcz, *Bridge Across Broken Time — Chinese and Jewish Cultural Memory*, New Haven and London, 1998.

35 Western and Indian Jews did, in contrast, demonstrate interest in the Jews of Kaifeng, at least from the late eighteenth century on. See Michael Pollak, *Mandarins, Jews and Missionaries — The Jewish Experience in the Chinese Empire*, 1st ed. 1980, 1st Weatherhill ed. New York-Tokyo, 1998, pp. 113-130.

36 Zhou Xun, *Chinese Perceptions of the "Jews" and Judaism. A History of the Youtai*, Richmond/Surrey, 2001, p.51.

37 Li Changlin, "The Present Day Chinese Attitude Towards Jews", *Points East*, Newsletter, Vol. 12, No. 3, November 1997, p. 11.

38 On Spinoza, see Historic Appendix at the end of this report.

39 The quotes were made at different times, the first (until "to this day") was written in 1924, see Xiao Xian, "An Overview of Chinese Impressions of and Attitudes toward Jews before 1949", *The Jews of China, Vol. 2, A Source Book and Research Guide*, ed. Jonathan Goldstein, New York-London, 1999, p. 38; the second was written in 1920, see Zhou Xun, op.cit., p. 57.

40 Irene Eber, "Chinese and Jews: Mutual Perceptions in Literary and Related Sources", *East-West Dialogue*, Vol. IV, No.2/Vol.V, No.1, June 2000, p. 217.

41 Lin Yutang, ed., *The Wisdom of Confucius*, New York, 1938, pp. 43-44.

42 See Edward Cody, "Shanghai Aims to Preserve Part of Its Jewish Legacy — Booming City is Likely to Save at Least Part of Neighbourhood Once Home to European Refugees", *The Washington Post*, 5 September 2004. This article,

and others on a gathering of former Jewish residents in Harbin on 2 September 2004 have appeared in general and Jewish newspapers.

43 Pan Guang, "The Development of Jewish and Israel Studies in China", *The Harry S. Truman Research Institute for the Advancement of Peace, Occasional Papers No.2*, The Hebrew University of Jerusalem, Spring 1992, pp. 5-6.

44 "Talmudist Meets Puzzled Jews in Russia's Far East", *Forward*, New York, 28 June 2002, p. 1.

45 Lewis S. Robinson, "The Bible in 20th Century Chinese Fiction", in Irene Eber, ed., *Bible in Modern China — The Literary and Intellectual Impact*, Monumenta Serica Monograph Series XLIII, Sankt Augustin, 1999, p. 253.

46 Ms. Lauren Katz, an American student in Beijing, conducted this survey from October to December 2003. The author followed the different stages of her research and has been authorised to use and quote the results as appropriate.

47 Merle Goldman, "A New Relationship between the Intellectuals and the State in the Post-Mao Period", *An Intellectual History of Modern China*, ed. M. Goldman et al., Cambridge MA., 2002, pp. 523, 537, 538.

48 Howard W. French, "China's leadership tries a fresh tactic: listening — Hu government consults intellectuals", *The New York Times*, 3 June 2004.

49 David Hale and Lyric Hughes Hale, "China Takes Off: China's Economic Explosion", *Foreign Affairs*, November/December 2003, p. 51.

50 Considered an elite university, RENMIN was created in 1950 at Mao Zedong's request, to train China's civil servants, including its future diplomats, from the working classes.

51 Xu Xin, "Some Thoughts On Our Policy Towards the Jewish Religion — Including A Discussion Of Our Policy Toward the Kaifeng Jews", in Roman Malek, ed., *Jews in China. From Kaifeng ... to Shanghai*, Monumenta Serica Monograph Series XLVI, Nettetal, 2000, p. 673.

52 For Mao Zedong, see Footnote 69. For Zhou Enlai, Israel Epstein reported an incident during one of Zhou's official visits to Poland, when the Chinese prime minister publicly showed his displeasure with the rising anti-Semitism of that country's Communist Party and government. See Israel Epstein, "On Being a Jew in China: A Personal Memoir", *The Jews of China*, Vol. 2, op.cit., p. 96.

53 Buddhism and the introduction of Buddhist monastic life to China represents a very different Chinese way, but monastic life in China has never touched more than a small minority.

54 Zhang Qianhong, "A Preliminary Discussion on Moses Mendelssohn's Enlightening Thought", *Studies in World Religions*, Chinese Academy of Social Sciences, Gen. No. 94, No. 3., 2003; idem, *Dilemma and Rebirth*, Beijing, 2003. Both in Chinese.

55 Prof. Fu Youde, University of Shandong, Jinan.

56 The works of Paul Cohen, Irene Eber, Merle Goldman, Jonathan Goldstein, Donald Leslie, Joseph Levenson, Benjamin Schwartz, and Vera Schwarcz, among others, address many of these questions.

57 Joseph Levenson, *Confucian China and its Modern Fate — The Problem of Intellectual Continuity*, Berkeley LA, 1958, p. 91.

58 Moshe Yeagar, "The Establishment of People's Republic of China-Israel Relations: Broader Implications for Southeast and South Asia", in *China and Israel — A Fifty Year Retrospective*, ed. Jonathan Goldstein, Westpoint/London, 1999, p. 128.

59 Prof. Suolao Wang, Beijing, interview of 24 October 2003.

60 P. Y. Saeki, *The Nestorian Documents and Relics in China*, 2nd edition, Tokyo, 1951. See particularly the "Jesus Messiah Sutra", pp. 223-224.

61 Hendrik Willem Van Loon, *The Story of the Bible*, Beijing, 1999, pp. 7, 179, 182, 183, 184. Needless

to say, the two quotations attributed to Jesus are quotes from the Jewish Bible. They are core principles of Rabbinic Judaism and one is an essential part of the daily prayers.

62 Prof. Zhou Xiefan, Beijing, interview of 23 October 2003.

63 Xiao Xian, op.cit., p. 41.

64 Dru C. Gladney, op. cit., p. 334.

65 See, for example, Yin Gang et al., *Arab-Israeli Conflicts: Issues and Solutions*, Chinese, Beijing, 2003.

 This book was sold out soon after it appeared.

66 Chiara Betta, "Myth and Memory. Chinese Portrayal of Silas Aaron Hardoon, Luo Jialing and the Aili Garden between 1924 and 1995", *Jews in China. From Kaifeng ... to Shanghai,* op.cit., p. 398.

67 David G. Goodman and Masanori Miyazawa, *Jews in the Japanese Mind — The History and Use of a Cultural Stereotype*, Lanham-Boulder-New York-Oxford, 2000, pp. 220 ff.

68 Xu Xin, "Chinese Policy Towards Judaism", paper presented at the *International Symposium Youtai — Presence and Perception of Jews and Judaism in China*, School of Applied Linguistics and Cultural Studies, Johannes Gutenberg University of Mainz, 19-23 September 2003, pp. 6, 7, 11, 12; reprinted in *Points East, Newsletter,* Vol. 19, March 2004, pp. 1, 3-7.

69 The absence of hostile attitudes is in line with some of Mao Zedong's brief comments from his early years, which are not only free of any anti-Semitism but show Mao's recognition of Jews and the "Jewish National Liberation Movement". See Stuart R. Schramm et al., eds., *Mao's Road to Power: Revolutionary Writings 1912-1949*, Armonk, NY, 1992, Vol. 1, pp. 337, 544; Vol. 2, p. 382.

70 Detailed reference to this symposium in footnote 68.

71 Prof. Ni Shixiong, FUDAN University, Shanghai, interview of 13 November 2003.

72 Ambassador (ret.) Lin Zhen, Beijing, interview of 28 October 2003.

73 Quotation from Xinhua News Agency.

74 Prof. Wang Jian, Shanghai Academy of Social Sciences, Centre of Jewish Studies, interview of 17 November 2003.

75 Ambassador (ret.) Lin Zhen, Beijing, interview of 28 October 2003.

76 Stephen C. Angle, *Human Rights and Chinese Thought — A Cross-Cultural Enquiry*, Cambridge UK, 2002, pp. 250-258.

77 Huang Lingyu, "Research on Judaism in China", *Jews in China. From Kaifeng ... to Shanghai*, op.cit., p.669.

78 Most Chinese students will buy a book that is not directly required for their studies if it costs no more then 10 yuan (1 US dollar = 8 yuan). A book that costs more than 15 yuan (or almost 2 dollars) is difficult to sell to students.

79 Liang Gong, "Twenty Years of Studies of Biblical Literature in the People's Republic of China (1976-1996)", *Bible in Modern China*, op.cit., p. 395.

80 Prof. Al Dien, President of the Sino-Judaic Institute, Menlo Park, interview of 31 March 2003 in New York.

81 Most of these students probably have no religion.

82 Of course, philosophy and Han ethnicity are not religions.

83 Beijing Foreign Studies University is considered China's first foreign language university and one of China's top universities. It offers courses in twenty-two foreign languages, the most popular being English. Hebrew is not offered, but there is an Arabic program.

84 Books include all kinds of books, textbooks too.

85 Students' replies "From class" were included in "Teachers".

86 These include family and friends.

87 The He Ping restaurant was an old Jewish restaurant in Shanghai.

88 These references are in the *Mishnah* and *Tossefta* (both completed in the second century C.E. but containing much earlier material), the *Sifra* and *Pesikta* (early and late *Midrash*), and also in the Babylonian and the Jerusalem Talmud. A useful and extensive compilation of these sources in Samuel Kraus, *Talmudische Altertümer*, Leipzig, 1910, pp. 140-141, 543-544.

89 Moshe Gil, *A History of Palestine, 634-1099*, Cambridge, New York, Port Chester, Melbourne, Sydney, 1992, p. 503.

90 Ph. Berger and M. Schwab, "Le plus ancien manuscrit Hébreu", *Journal Asiatique*, Onzième Série, Tome II, Paris, 1913, p. 165. Translation by the author.

91 William Charles White, *Chinese Jews*, 2nd ed., reprint, Toronto, 1966, pp. 8, 45.

92 Salomon Wald, *Chinese Jews in European Thought*, paper presented at the International Symposium "Youtai — Presence and Perception of Jews and Judaism in China", School of Applied Linguistics and Cultural Studies, Johannes Gutenberg University of Mainz, 19-23 September 2003, pp. 8-10.

93 Spinoza, "The Theological-Political Tractate", *Complete Works* with translations by S. Shirley, ed. and Michael L. Morgan, Indianapolis/Cambridge, 2002, p. 425.

94 Marcus N. Adler, "Chinese Jews", London, 1900, *Jews in Old China — Some Western Views*, ed. Hyman Kublin, New York, 1971, p. 94.

For Perlman, see S. M. Perlman, "The History of the Jews in China", London, 1909, ibid. p. 167 ff.

95 Irene Eber, "A Critical Survey of Classical Chinese Literary Works in Hebrew", *One Into Many — Translation and Dissemination of Classical Chinese Literature*, ed. Leo Tak-hung Chan, Amsterdam-New York, 2003, p. 303.

96 Irene Eber, *Sinim ve'Yehudim, Mifgashim ben Tarbuyoth* ("Chinese and Jews — Encounters Between Cultures"), Jerusalem, 2002.

Recently, Prof. Eber discovered political, cultural, and literary articles on China in Yiddish newspapers of pre-World War II Poland. These include translations of Chinese poetry, by writers who perished without leaving a name (oral communication). The Yiddish-speaking public's interest in China must have been considerable.

97 Chang Shoou-Huey, "China und Jiddisch-Jiddische Kultur in China, Chinesische Literatur auf Jiddisch", *Jews in China. From Kaifeng ... to Shanghai*, op.cit., p. 487. Translation by the author.

98 Cella-Margaretha Girardet, *Jüdische Mäzene für die Preussischen Museen zu Berlin*, Engelsbach/Frankfurt/Washington, 1997, p. 101.

99 *Ausstellung Chinesischer Kunst*, Gesellschaft für Ostasiatische Kunst und Preussische Akademie der Künste, Berlin, 1929.

100 Rebecca Bitterman, ed., *China: One Hundred Treasures*, Jerusalem, 2001.

101 The painter Shen Hao (circa 1630-1650) gave this title to an album of his landscape paintings. Museum Rietberg, *Tausend Gipfel und Zehntausend Täler-Chinesische Malerei aus der Sammlung C.A. Drenowatz*, Zürich, 1983, Fig. 21.

102 Benjamin I. Schwartz, "History and Culture in the Thought of Joseph Levenson", Maurice Meissner and Roads Murphy, eds., *The Mozartian Historian, Essays on the Works of Joseph R. Levenson*, Berkeley-Los Angeles-London, 1976, p. 101.

103 Paul Cohen, *Discovering History in China — American Historical Writing on the Recent Chinese Past*, New York, 1984, pp. 150-151.